REST
STOPS
FOR THE
SOUL

REST STOPS FOR THE SOUL

A Guide
for Traveling
the Trail of Transformation

Joseph Nassal, CPPS

FOREST OF PEACE
Publishing

Suppliers for the Spiritual Pilgrim

Rest Stops for the Soul

copyright © 1998, by Joseph Nassal

Library of Congress Cataloging-in-Publication Data

Nassal, Joe, 1955-
    Rest stops for the soul : a guide for traveling the trail of transformation / Joseph Nassal.
        p.   cm.
    ISBN 0-939516-38-1 (pbk.)
    1.—Religious life—Catholic Church. I. Title.
BX2350.2.N34   1998
248. 4'82—dc21   97-51482
                                                             CIP

published by

Forest of Peace Publishing, Inc.
PO Box 269
Leavenworth, KS 66048-0269   USA
1-800-659-3227

printed by

Hall Directory, Inc.
Topeka, KS 66608-0348

1st printing: January 1998

FOR

FATHER ED HAYS,

storyteller and sage,
priest, poet and prophet,
soul friend for the ages
and founder of
Shantivanam,
a sacred rest stop
for the soul

Great are the myths . . .
I too delight in them,
Great are Adam and Eve . . .
I too look back and accept them;
Great the risen and fallen nations,
and their poets,
women, sages, inventors,
rulers, warriors, and priests.

Walt Whitman
Leaves of Grass

CONTENTS

SOUL MUSIC

I want to sing
of poets and prophets,
clowns and kings;
of sages and saints,
wisdom and wings.

I want to stay
in caves covered in clover,
listen to mountains pray,
ponds moan, meadows groan
and fields play.

I want to make music
only souls can hear
in a place of stillness
we draw dangerously near.

With lyrics so rare
we gather to learn
who we are
and so much more.

I want to play new music
on an old lyre
and find my answer
by the window or the fire.
Here new dreams are conceived,
then consumed in a crematorium
for a new creation.

I want to sing a new community
not build one;
songs shall be the stones,
and when all the songs are sung,
we'll write some more.

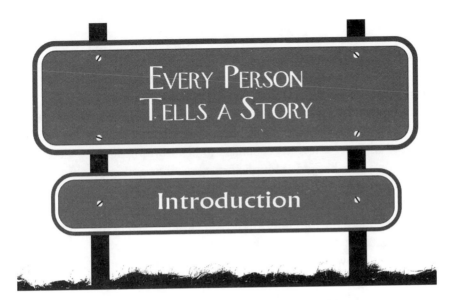

EVERY PERSON TELLS A STORY

Introduction

Afoot and light-hearted I take
to the open road,
Healthy, free, the world
before me.

— Walt Whitman

A story must be told in such a way that it constitutes help in itself. My grandfather was lame. Once they asked him to tell a story about his teacher. And he related how his teacher used to hop and dance while he prayed. My grandfather rose as he spoke, and he was so swept away by his story that he began to hop and dance to show how the master had done it. From that hour he was cured of his lameness. That's how to tell a story.

— Martin Buber

There is a place on Interstate 35 in Iowa called Story City. Really! I once stopped at a fast food restaurant there on my way back to Kansas City. I was minding my own business when an older gentleman unable to find a table asked if he could sit across from me. My mouth full of food, I waved my hand to show him he was welcome at the table. Since we were strangers, I figured he would be a silent guest and would not interrupt my solitude in the midst of the crowded room. Little did I know he was the unofficial mayor of this mystical, maybe even magical, place known as Story City.

He sat down and began to tell me that he had been clipping hedges all morning and his arms were tired. I consoled him by saying that at least it was a nice day to be outdoors. Normally, talking about the weather is as deep as conversation ever gets with a stranger. But not for the "mayor" of Story City. My response to his morning activity gave him an opening. He barged through this open door and made himself at home. He told me he had just returned from visiting his brother in Texas. One day, his brother took him to a flea market where he met a man with whom he talked for four hours before his brother had to drag him out of the store. "That guy was like an old friend I hadn't seen in years," he said. "You know how there are people like that? People who just sit down and start talking and you think you'd known them for years even though you just met them?"

I nodded since I was having lunch with one of those people.

As the man continued to talk, he told me that he worked at a rest stop on the interstate. "I really enjoy working there," he said. "You meet all kinds of interesting people. Most of them are tired from driving all day, so I just tell them a little story they can take with them the rest of the way. A little fuel for their souls, if you will."

This old gentleman had it right. Stories are fuel for our souls. We fill each other's souls with the high octane energy of our life experiences. From sitting down at the family table and telling stories of what happened at work or school to recalling landmark moments of birth and death and other rites of passage, we are all storytellers. We may not be professional or poetic when we tell these tales, but we are passionate. For these are the stories that shape our lives.

On the road of life, stories are the rest stops for the soul. Like the unofficial mayor of Story City told me, without stories and the chance to share them, we all run out of gas. And for many in our world today, the indicator is dangerously close to empty.

Have you had this experience? You have been driving for a long time along a lonely stretch of road. You sense the ache in your back as your eyelids try to draw the curtains on the windows to your soul. The wheels of the car veer to the right, hitting the shoulder bumps. Startled, you jump into wakefulness for a moment, roll down the window and turn up the radio, but nothing seems to help. Before long, your head bobs again. When you are aware of such fatigue, it's time to stop at a rest area and perhaps drink some coffee, catch some fresh air, stretch your legs.

And visit Story City:

Once upon a time, there was a man who was weary of life. He was tired to death, so he decided to leave his home, his family and friends to search for Story City, where everything would be different — new, full and rewarding. On his journey, he spent the night in a forest. When he settled down for the evening, he took a sandwich he had prepared and an apple out his knapsack and had a bite to eat. Before he went to sleep, he was careful to take off his shoes and point them in the new direction he wanted to take.

As he slept, however, an angel appeared. Unknown to the weary traveler, the angel turned his shoes around.

The next morning when he awoke, he stepped into his shoes and continued his journey toward what he thought was Story City. A few days later he came to this destination of his dreams. It was not quite as large as he had imagined it. In fact, it looked rather familiar. He found a familiar street and knocked on a familiar door. When the door opened, his family was there to welcome him home. He lived happily ever after.

The story of the man weary of life helps us understand why we need places where we can take off our shoes and rest awhile within the pages of our own life's story. We need those spaces in our lives that allow God to point our feet in a new direction. It is a direction, more often than not, which leads us back to each other.

STORIES: IN TOUCH WITH OUR TRUTH

This book is an attempt to articulate a language of the soul. There's a question that guides this exploration: How do people of faith become transforming agents of the holy in the world? The answer I propose is that by staying in touch with the stories that shape our lives, we touch our deepest truth. By paying attention to the stories we are telling now and by creating new stories that flow from the dreams we hold for ourselves, our children and our world, we walk the trail of transformation. There is mystery and magic written in between the lines of our mythical and mystical lives. By taking the risk to recall our own experiences of pain and promise, we clarify our commitment to be more human. By reflecting in our conversations our own understanding and experience of faith and all that it entails, we set ourselves on the road to be more holy and more alive.

When we hear the word "myth," our first inclination is to think of fairy tales. We recall stories we heard in grammar school that captured our imagination "once upon a time" but are irrelevant in an age of reason and practicality. Santa Claus, for example, is a sacred myth. As children, we believe in the presence of this jolly and gentle saint who symbolizes a spirit of generosity and compassion. When we reach a certain age, though we no longer believe in the factual existence of Santa Claus, we still cling to the truths the sacred story conveys.

There is a difference between a "true" story and a "truth" story. A "true" story reflects an actual event. It is factual but may or may not reflect an inner or deeper truth. A "truth" story may not be based on an actual event and may not give all the facts of a particular incident. Yet in its telling, it conveys meaning and reflects a truth about the human condition.

Myths are the truths upon which our personal and communal lives are built. Myths are the soul stories that have shaped us and continue to sustain us. Without these soul stories, we might be very factual, but we won't be very faithful. Without these myths, we might be very professional, but we won't be very passionate. Without stories, our heads might thrive, but our hearts will shrivel and die. Statistics inform the mind; stories form, inform, and transform the soul. Stories spark and reflect the imagination, and as Albert Einstein once said, "Imagination is more important than knowledge."

When we enter this "nation of images," the imagination, we become the guardians of sacred stories that help us articulate our experiences of God. But soul stories also take us beyond what is being said at the moment of speaking to the place in the soul where the person saying the words finds his or her life meaningful. When we take the time to share the stories of our lives, the truths we have learned from the sheer experience of living, we become "soul-journers," companions of the soul who discover in the telling of our stories those uncommon truths found in our common experiences. These stories help us to make sacred connections that remind us that we do not walk alone.

The basic premise of *Rest Stops for the Soul* is that we are transformed by these mythic tales and made sacred by our own stories.

This book seeks to tap the innate potential in each of us to be poets of our own primary truth. As we grow in this holy personal identity, we gather with others to share these stories that have shaped us. In an atmosphere of tenderness and trust, this truth-telling nurtures courage in us to embrace our common identity as ministers of myth and messengers of truth. Part of my reality is that although I presently live in a cabin in the woods and am director of a contemplative house of prayer, life on the road appeals to me. Though I may have a contemplative heart, I also have missionary feet. Mobility has meaning for me. My life has been a winding road with more than a few rest stops along the way. Though the temptation is always there to look forward to the next stop around the bend, the stories I've heard at these rest stops along the road of life have taught me that the truth is not so much found in facts as in the stories. Whether the facts of a particular story are correct is not necessarily important. What is important is this: Does the story bring us home to our own truth?

There are three kinds of stories central to our reflection: those of creation, incarnation and redemption. Creation stories remind us of the roots of our faith. Incarnation stories reveal the dreams of the divine in our very human lives. Redemption stories reflect the process of finding the wings of possibility beneath our feet as we walk this trail of transformation. We need all three. We need to know from where we have come. We need to see how God is active in our lives right now. We need to embrace the truths that will ultimately set us free to become the people we are called and destined to be.

That old man I met in Story City was right. When the ache of driving all day along the highway called holiness becomes more than we can bear; when the road becomes so rough that the bumps we hit bruise our souls; when the roadblocks and detours we encounter fuel our frustration; when we are weary of the road and weary of life, it's time to take a break. The road sign informs us, **Rest Stop: One Mile**. It's time to rest awhile.

This book invites us to remember that even if there is no rest stop for miles, we can always pull over on the side of the road to rest on God's shoulder. In this pause that refreshes our souls, we listen to those sacred stories of both pain and promise from our past, present and future that shape our lives and show us our destiny.

Rest Stop

The Experience of Transformation

We are not converted only once in our lives, but many times. And this endless series of large and small conversions, these inner revolutions, leads to our transformation in Christ.

– Thomas Merton

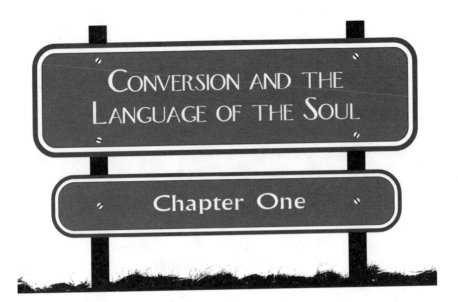

CONVERSION AND THE LANGUAGE OF THE SOUL

Chapter One

Come to the edge, he said.
They said, "We are afraid"
Come to the edge, he said.
They came.
He pushed them . . . And they flew.

– Guillaume Apollinaire

Draw your chair up close to the edge of the precipice and I'll tell
you a story.

– F. Scott Fitzgerald

As a young boy, I remember camping out with classmates and sitting around the fire late at night. Every sound seemed magnified in the darkness, creating an absolutely eerie atmosphere for telling ghost stories. Each of us tried to top the previous storyteller in terms of gruesome details or sheer terror. Often these stories kept us awake all night for fear that if we'd fall asleep one or another of the ghosts might appear.

The ghost story is a genre designed to keep us awake. Soul stories keep us awake and *alive*. They are told in an atmosphere of reverence and delight, not to eclipse a previous story but to connect each one's experience and thereby discover we are not alone. Like children drawing lines in a coloring book to connect the dots, finding at the finish the image of a person who looks familiar, soul stories scan the stars in the night sky to remind us that we are a precious part of a greater whole, that we are children of the universe. As that word "universe" implies, each of us is "one verse" of a greater story linked by the love of those who have gone before us, the love of those around us, the love of those who will come after us and, most profoundly, the love of God. In concert with all of creation, we share these stories to know who we are, why we are here, to whom we belong and where we are going.

So often in our lives we are lulled to sleep by the routine. We fall into ruts and grow comfortable in those narrow spaces and places of our lives. We sleepwalk through our days and sleep too soundly at night even to dream. But in the language of the soul, conversion is the alarm clock ringing in our hearts. It shakes us, startles us, wakes us up to the reality of God's abiding presence in our lives.

To fully experience this presence of love, however, we must be fully awake. In this chapter we reflect on certain experiences, certain events, certain surprises — certain stories of the soul — that awaken us to the deepest dreams and desires and truth of our souls and call us to a deeper communion with God, with others, with all of creation.

Turning Points of Transformation

The experience of conversion implies change. Recently I was visiting a parish where I previously had been assigned. One elderly woman, whom I had not seen since I left the parish almost a ten years before, greeted me with a wide smile. I said, "Mary, you haven't changed a bit!"

To which she replied, "You mean I looked this bad ten years ago?"

We are always changing. If we are not, we're dead. I'm not referring so much to physical changes that occur in and on our bodies as we grow older as to the experience of spiritual transformation that describes our soul's inner yearning and turning toward God. As Thomas Merton said:

We are not converted only once in our lives, but many times. And this endless series of large and small conversions, these inner revolutions, leads to our transformation in Christ.

The kind of transformation I'm talking about here is found in this story: It was First Communion Sunday in the parish. The girls were dressed in their white cotton dresses with lace veils; the boys had on their dark blue suits, white shirts and ties. Their eyes were full of excitement and anticipation, their bodies filled with nervous energy as they tried to no avail to sit still in the pews. The moment they had been waiting for was about to take place. After almost a year of studying about Holy Communion in their second grade religion class; after watching all the older children go up to receive Communion during the all-school liturgies; after being left behind in the pews by their parents when the time for Communion arrived, now they were ready to take their place at the table. Of course they didn't understand the deep theological significance of what they were about to receive — after all, they were only in second grade. But they knew it was important, and everyone in the church could sense their excitement.

When they came up, one by one, to receive the Eucharist for the first time, one little girl kept looking over her shoulder. Her mom and dad were divorced. Her father had moved to another town and had not been back to see the family for some time. But her mother was in the back of church. The girl kept looking for her. That morning, her mother told me later, the little girl had said, "Mommy, I sure wish you could receive Communion with me."

That was the turning point. The little girl's wish would change the woman's life. She came back to the church she had left when her husband left her. She had been brought up to believe that divorce was fatal in the eyes of the church. She was an outcast and did not feel welcome. Now, however, through her daughter's First Communion, she came home.

The little girl's wish became an invitation and an action. In the words of her daughter, the mother found God grasping her by the hand and guiding her from the fear and guilt that had led her to isolation and alienation toward the hospitality and hopefulness that now were leading her back to the table of Communion.

This is the language of the soul that expresses the experience of conversion. Sometimes small, seemingly insignificant events — maybe a word from a child or a prayer from a friend — set the stage for our continuing transformation within God's abiding presence. Sometimes it's a feeling, unsettling and inarticulate, that has been gnawing at our insides like teeth through a rope. It may be a feeling that grows, mysterious and silent, until one day it erupts into an action.

Dorothy Day, the founder of the Catholic Worker movement, recalls in her autobiography why she had her daughter baptized even though she herself wasn't Catholic at the time. "I felt it was the greatest gift I could do for my child," she writes. Even though it cost Dorothy the man she loved, this powerful feeling inside moved her to bring her daughter to the waters of baptism. She felt that belonging to a faith community would bring order into her daughter's life — an order which her own life had lacked.

Sometimes a soul message is passed on from child to parent, as it was in that daughter looking over her shoulder before she received her First Communion. Sometimes it is a gift from parent to child, as it was for Dorothy Day. However conversion happens, it is always a deeply personal experience that leads one to community. It begins in the heart of an individual and moves that person to the heart of community.

That woman whose daughter made her First Communion had been thinking for a long time that she should go back to church. She wanted to. She missed Mass. Not in the sense we normally think of in the Roman Catholic tradition or hear in the Sacrament of Penance: "Forgive me, Father, for I have sinned; I missed Mass on Sunday." There the meaning is: I skipped Mass, or I couldn't make it because I was out of town. But did we really *miss* Mass? Did we miss being there? Did we miss the experience of Eucharist in the same way we'd miss visiting with an old friend? That was this woman's experience. She was absent most Sundays from the Communion table, and she really missed being there. Yet until her daughter wished that they could receive Communion together that morning, she didn't realize how much she missed the Eucharist.

A child's innocent question, a death of a loved one, a welcome by a stranger, a telephone call from a long-forgotten friend — these experiences reflect the soul speaking to us. Now, suddenly, what didn't matter yesterday has become of primary importance today.

For many of us, when we think about conversion, the model is St. Paul being knocked off his horse. It's a flash of lightening, a thunderbolt out of nowhere that throws us for a loop and turns our world upside down. But more often than not, our conversion to a deeper relationship with our God happens in small steps and natural ways. For most of us, conversion is not a once-in-a-lifetime occurrence. Rather it is an ongoing experience of being shaken or startled or awakened by occurrences or stories written in the language of the soul, awakened to a reality that for some time has been on the fringe of our mind or memory.

PIECES OF A PUZZLE

Recently I was giving a retreat at a convent where a number of retired sisters live. In one of the recreation rooms there was a large table set up with the beginning of a puzzle on the top of it. It was a large puzzle with thousands of pieces. As the picture on the box showed, it was an especially challenging puzzle. It was a nature scene with lots of greens and browns and whites for snow-capped mountains in the distance and blues for the sky and the river that ran through a valley. Whenever a sister found the time or was motivated, she would spend a few minutes working on the puzzle.

The puzzle metaphor gives us a clue into the process of conversion. We have the picture before us, a picture of what it will look like when it all comes together. But it takes time. Each piece of the puzzle is unique. One cannot force a piece into a place where it doesn't fit. We have to work on it. We have to be patient with the process. Over time, however, by working alone and sometimes with others, the puzzle comes together. For Dorothy Day, having her child baptized was the last piece of her conversion puzzle. Shortly after that, she became Catholic herself.

Conversion begins as a deeply personal experience. Pursuing the puzzle metaphor, imagine a little girl faced with the task of putting together a puzzle of the world. She tries and tries to make all the pieces fit together, but not being familiar with some of Earth's territory, she becomes frustrated by the lack of progress. Then her mother comes along and says, "Turn the puzzle over." On the other side of the puzzle is a picture of the little girl's face. Knowing very well what she looks like, the girl puts that picture of her face together. When she turns the puzzle over again, the whole world is put together.

This is perhaps the best place to begin: with ourselves. Before we can seek to change the world, we must first be open to accepting ourselves: our limits and our fears, our yearnings and our tears, our gifts and our goals, our loves and our losses.

If we have ever grasped for something for a long time without being able to reach it; if we have looked for something for a long time without being able to find it; if we have ever longed for something or someone for a long time without being able to fulfill our longing, then we stand on the threshold of transformation. We are ready for conversion.

First, though, we have to work on the pieces of our own puzzle.

Maybe there are some pieces that have been misplaced or put aside because of a fear of "needing to have it all together." Conversely, some of us may think that because our sin is always before us we certainly don't want to appear to others as if we have our act together. If we all thought like this, however, nothing would ever happen. The point of conversion is that something does indeed happen. What happens is this: We accept ourselves for who we are — fragile and fearful and fraught with missing pieces — and through the grace of God we are given a vision of what the whole puzzle looks like.

FEELING THE PULSE OF OUR PASSION

On this trail of transformation, we must stop now and then to tell the stories of our faith and our fear. At these rest stops, we create an environment where we are free to make mistakes and free to ask questions.

In the language of the soul, the experience of conversion is like that commercial for *Corn Flakes*: "Taste them again for the first time." We've tried all sorts of other cereals that promise to be more exciting or more nourishing or more filling or less filling, and so we forgot how good those simple corn flakes taste.

Conversion is what has been brewing on the back burner for a long time. Somehow, some way, someone turns up the heat, and what had been simmering now boils over. It gets our attention. We have to act.

Conversion is the experience that pushes us to that moment when we have to decide to either turn down the heat or dish out the soup.

What conversion teaches us is that we don't have all the answers. But the soul tries to show us that if we are willing to live the questions like sojourners in a strange land, like pilgrims plodding toward a promised land, we will begin to live the questions into answers. As Antonio Machado tells us:

> Traveler, there is no path.
> Paths are made by walking.

When we walk with the questions, a passion will emerge that will propel us on the path of conversion, and our life story will be punctuated with that passion.

For many of us, however, our journey of faith resembles something that great philosopher, Yogi Berra, once said: We come to the fork in the road and we take it. Sometimes, instead of traveling one path or the other, we just stand there and our pilgrim's progress is stopped by indecision.

Stuck in the fork in the road, we learn that one of the important words in the language of the soul is passion. The word evokes deep feeling. When we speak of the passion of Jesus Christ, for example, the implication is that Jesus felt so deeply for humanity that he was willing to die to free us from our slavery to sin and our dance with despair.

What do we feel passionate about in our lives?

One way of answering that question is to ask another: What am I alive to? What makes me feel alive? Who are the people, what are the hobbies, what are the experiences that make me come alive? Too often we just go through the motions. One day ends and another begins, and nothing changes. We see those same sights on the way to work every morning. We are people who wear our gray, flannel suits on the inside.

Conversion implies passion, the kind of passion reflected in an episode of M*A*S*H (perhaps the most prolific television series, in terms of mythic tales, ever made). The story concerns a young soldier, an accomplished pianist, who is injured in the war. He loses his right hand and will never again be able to play the piano. Dr. Winchester, the M*A*S*H unit's brilliant but arrogant surgeon from Boston, encourages the young soldier not to give up or give in to his disability. He finds some classical music pieces written specifically for the left hand. But the soldier is not moved; he does not want to become, in his words, "some kind of freak pianist." Finally, Winchester tells him: "David, don't you understand that you have a gift? I can play the piano. I can play the notes. But I never had the gift to make the music. Oh, as a surgeon, I can make a scalpel sing, but what I wanted more than anything in the world was to play the piano. But I was never given that gift. You have it, and though you may not be able to use one of your hands, you can use the gift to teach, to write, to conduct. You have the passion."

Passion is that driving force that pulses within us from the very center of our being. When we find our passion, we find ourselves. We find who we are in God's heart. We discover our true vocation in life. Passionate people are those who have the eyes of their hearts focused on a single goal, a solitary dream, a spectacular view. They never lose sight of others around them, but they know what they must do and who they must be to achieve a sense of being whole.

Though David had lost his hand and so could no longer play the piano, Dr. Winchester sought to awaken in him the gift, the passion, that begins not with our hands but with our hearts. David sustained a wound and his hand was amputated, but the surgeon could never amputate David's passion unless David willed it, unless David allowed the passion to die within him.

Along the trail of our own transformation we all have met people with such passion. For us to understand the language of the soul, however, we must discover our own passion. Being in touch with the passion of our life opens us to the essence of our soul. It reflects the knowledge of self, of knowing who we are in God's eyes and in our own.

Such knowledge is brought out in one of my favorite stories. It's about a group of people who gathered one day after church services to have coffee and doughnuts and enjoy each other's company. Somehow, the conversation came around to memory, and a young man in the group said he had memorized the Twenty-Third Psalm as a child and had never forgotten it. So the others encouraged him to recite the psalm, "The Lord is my shepherd, there is nothing I shall want," which he did, flawlessly.

An older gentlemen listened to the young man recite the psalm. When the applause for the young man's talent had died down, this old man began to recite the same psalm. As those gathered listened to the old man say the words, they began to weep softly. When the old man finished, there was not applause but absolute silence. A person tapped the young man on the shoulder and whispered, "What just happened?" The young man replied, "Isn't it obvious? I know the psalm, but this man knows the shepherd."

The difference between mediocrity and genius; the difference between saying prayers and praying; the difference between making a living and living with passion is found in that story about the young man and the elderly gentleman reciting the words to the Twenty-Third Psalm. The difference is that some of us are content with memorizing or knowing about God's Word while others of us desire more than anything in life to know God.

We certainly come to know the divine through God's Word, which is the map for living this adventure we call life. On the trail of transformation, however, we are encouraged to awaken to the reality of God not just by reading the map but also by listening to the language of the soul in the stories of the people we meet along the way.

Feeling the passion of this present moment affords us the courage to not be afraid of making a mistake or looking foolish in the world's eyes. If we fear falling or failing or tripping over mistakes, nothing will ever happen. If, however, we are passionate about life and our place in the unfolding plan of God's salvation for our world, we will respond with wide open hearts and ready hands to do what we can and must to bring the world to the threshold of transformation.

The result of listening to the language of the soul is that we come alive again. We notice things. We recognize people. We see with new eyes and, even more importantly, with new hearts. We do not give in to routine but are willing to transform the sameness of our lives with the spark of passion.

At the rest stops of the soul, our challenge is to be ready to be changed by the movement of God's Spirit in our lives. Be ready to be moved by the words of a song or a film or a friend. Be ready to be changed by the question of a child or the memory of a senior citizen. In all of these and more the soul is speaking, and we are invited to listen, look, live, taste, touch and smell the presence of God in our midst. We are encouraged to open our senses to the wonders of life that are happening right now.

An Epiphany at the Camel Stop Cafe

The readiness for change in our lives makes us aware of another important word in the language of the soul: epiphany. The original meaning of this strange-sounding word is "manifestation." More specifically, it is a manifestation of the Divine Presence. When our senses are open and we are fully awake and aware, the likelihood of receiving an epiphany is quite high. On the morning of her First Communion, that little girl's question to her mother offered her mom an epiphany. Dr. Winchester's advice to the young soldier who lost his hand and thought he had lost his passion set the stage for an epiphany. The old gentleman's rendition of the Twenty-Third Psalm that moved those who heard it to a sacred stillness provided a manifestation of God's presence, an epiphany.

On our own spiritual journeys, it is necessary that we stop now and then to recall sacred moments when the presence of the Divine One has become very real to us. Those moments are epiphanies because they shake us out of the doldrums while awakening us to new dreams.

The story from Scripture we often associate with the word epiphany is the tale of the three kings (sometimes referred to as wise men or astrologers) from the East who come to pay homage to a baby in Bethlehem. We are familiar with this incarnation story because it has become a traditional tale we tell around Christmas time. These three kings have inspired yuletide carols and famous Christmas stories like O. Henry's "The Gift of the Magi." Besides reflecting the ancient truth about the birth of Jesus as a "light to all nations," a divine manifestation of God's love for all people, the story also suggests certain truths about our own journey of transformation. For example, what do we do when we lose our sense of direction on this soulful journey of transformation? We are familiar with the story of how the three astrologers stopped at King Herod's court in Jerusalem and asked for directions. But do we know the story of the night before the three wise men from the East arrived at Herod's place?

When the star seekers were in sight of the bright lights of the big city of Jerusalem, they pulled their caravan off the road at a place known as Camel Stop Cafe for food and refueling.

As their servants took care of the camels, the three astrologers went inside the big tent for dinner. After ordering their food, the three astrologers took out their maps to check their bearings. One picked up a spoon to show the other two their precise location. The spoon was greasy. (Yes, you guessed it, the Camel Stop Cafe was the original "greasy spoon.") Balthasar wiped the spoon on his cloak, pointed to their present location and said to the other two, "Once we get to Jerusalem, my friends, I don't have a clue as to where we go from there."

Melchior, the somber one, said, "I guess we'll have to stop in Jerusalem for directions."

"You've got to be kidding!" Gaspar chided. "What will our wives say?"

"What do you mean?"

"I mean they're always getting after us because we think we're so wise that we never have to stop and ask for directions."

"We have no choice," Balthasar said. "We've been following this star for a long time, and we certainly seem to be getting close. But it's evident from our projections that the star is not over Jerusalem as we had originally calculated. And since we're from the East and not familiar with this these wide-open spaces in the West, we'll need someone who knows the local landscape to guide us the rest of the way."

"Balthasar is right," Melchior said. "We need help. Once we get to Jerusalem we'll stop for directions."

As Madge, their waitress, brought out their dinner, Gaspar nudged Balthasar and whispered, "Maybe she can help us. After all, what better place to get directions and road conditions than a camel stop?"

Balthasar shrugged. "Excuse me, miss," he said. "We're from out of town."

"No kidding," Madge replied. "I could tell that by the way you dress. Didn't you see everyone looking at you when you came in the tent?"

"We're used to that," Melchior shrugged. "Anyway, we were wondering if you could help us. For many days now we've been following this star. Have you noticed it?"

"Can't say that I have," Madge said. "But then I work the late shift so I don't get off work until dawn. No time for star gazing, if you know what I mean."

"Yes, well," Balthasar cleared his throat. "We understand. But, you see, this star is the most remarkable astrological sign we've ever seen in all our years of experience. According to our research, it signifies the birth of a king. And we want to pay our respects. We initially expected the star to be directly over the holy city of Jerusalem, but we have now concluded that the star is resting over a place somewhere south of the city. Do you know that area?"

"Naw, can't say that I do." However, Madge said she'd check with the cook, who she thought had grown up somewhere south of Jerusalem.

While she went to check with the cook, the three astrologers enjoyed their dinner. At one point, Gaspar said, "You know, it's been bugging me since we left that you two wise guys have brought gifts for this newborn king and I didn't bring a thing."

Melchior shook his head to indicate his displeasure with his absentminded colleague. But Balthasar said, "Not a problem. Look, this camel stop has a gift shop. Maybe you can pick up something here."

"But what does one buy a newborn king?"

"If you had done your homework," Melchior said, "you wouldn't be in this predicament. Both Balthasar and I studied the Scriptures and discovered the prophecy of Isaiah which says, 'Caravans of camels shall fill you, dromedaries from Midian and Ephah; all from Sheba shall come bearing gold and frankincense.' So, naturally, I brought gold and Balthasar brought the frankincense."

Gaspar sighed. "Yah, but according to that prophecy the two of you have covered both bases. What should I bring?"

"Maybe you could leave behind one of your camels," Balthasar suggested.

"Naw, I can't spare a camel. I'll need all of them for the ride back. As you've noticed, we haven't run into many camel stops in this long stretch of wasteland. I'll just check out the gift shop; maybe I can find something fit for a king."

"Good luck," Melchior said as he wiped his spoon with his napkin.

When Madge brought the check, she told the astrologers that no one had noticed the star they were talking about and the cook was too busy to give her a lesson in geography. As Balthasar and Melchior got up to leave the tent, Gaspar came from the gift shop.

"Well, what did you get?" Balthasar asked.

"Myrrh," Gaspar smiled. "It was on sale — 50% off!"

Melchior grumbled. "You're going to give myrrh to a child? Are you out of your mind?"

"Why, what's wrong with myrrh? It has a nice smell to it." Gaspar held the bottle under Melchior's nose.

"You fool!" Melchior said, brushing away the bottle. "Myrrh is used in these parts to anoint a body for burial. You're going to give a newborn child a gift that will remind his parents of death."

"Don't worry about it," Balthasar said. "I'm sure Jerusalem has a lot of fine shops. When we pass through there tomorrow, you can pick up something else. Come on, it's time we get some sleep. We have a long day tomorrow. There's no telling how much farther we have to ride after we stop in Jerusalem for directions."

WISDOM: ASKING FOR DIRECTIONS

Well, as Paul Harvey might say, we know the rest of the story because we hear it every year on the feast of Epiphany. Yet when we couple the little known part of the tale — the astrologers' conversation at the Camel Stop Cafe — with the more familiar Gospel story, certain truths about our own spiritual sojourn surface for our soulful exploration.

For example, though we have come to call these three magi from the East "wise men," if they were so wise, why did they have to stop and ask for directions? Perhaps the answer lies in our understanding that these astrologers, though very well versed about signs that appeared in the night sky, were less familiar with the signs posted on earth. They needed help.

Perhaps this is the beginning of wisdom: being humble enough to stop and ask for directions. Rather than getting ourselves hopelessly lost by only looking at the stars in the sky, perhaps the truly wise look also for signs of God's manifestation in the eyes and hearts of those they encounter along the way. Being wise men and women does not mean having all the answers or even knowing where we're going all the time. Being wise means being willing to ask the right questions and trust in the goodness of those we meet along the way.

When we seek someone out for spiritual direction, for example, do we look for someone who seems to know all the answers? Or do we look for someone wise enough to realize that he or she is also on the journey? Someone who will walk with us for a while and be our companion rather than our guide. As a companion, the wise one who accompanies us will at times be able to point out certain obstacles along the way, but only because he or she has taken this journey inward and so has been here before. Wise companions may not know exactly where our obstacles and hazards and dead ends might be, but they have found some of their own. They will thus be in a position to ask the right questions that will give us a new sense of direction in our own star search.

Like our three astrologers in the story, they are humble enough to admit that they are lost at times, and so they will ask someone they believe might offer them some advice — someone like Madge who has been around and knows her own truth. Someone who spends her life in service of others, even if she doesn't find much time to gaze at the stars. Someone who works the night shift, who is not afraid of the dark, and is humble enough to admit what she doesn't know and will go ask someone else. True wisdom lies in being open to the truth that all peoples might give to us as we journey in faith.

At the same time, the story also suggests that we be careful about just whom we ask for directions. When they arrived in Jerusalem, the astrologers stopped at Herod's palace. Perhaps they thought that if anyone would know the directions to the birthplace of the newborn king, it would be the one presently sitting on the throne as king of Israel.

Of course, as "king" of Israel, Herod had no real power since he was more or less a puppet of the Roman government who pulled the strings. He had a safe, comfortable position from which he could exploit the people and build his reputation and prestige on the backs of those he oppressed. That is why it is not surprising that he was threatened when these astrologers showed up and told him about the star and the birth of a "new king." This child was destined to give the very people Herod was oppressing cause for hope. Naturally, Herod didn't need that, so he tried to lure the astrologers into serving as covert agents to find this threat to his power. This is how people of darkness operate — this is their mode of operation — they use others to promote their own devious designs for destruction.

So the story suggests that we be careful whom we ask for directions. Herod was an enemy of hope. In a story that reflects the radiance of God's light for all peoples, Herod symbolizes the dark side of life. He is the shadow that seeks to smother the light. Though we need people on our spiritual journey who are not afraid of their own shadows and who have some experience of walking in the dark, we must be careful that these people are not like Herod: people who love the darkness and are afraid of the light, people who look at the world through dark shades of cynicism and despair.

On our journey, we are not to be afraid of these shadowy figures but to realize that as sojourners who search for the light, these night stalkers will always be there to offer advice. We must be realistic enough to know that not everyone navigates by the same dreams for peace, for justice, for freedom. There are still Herods hovering in our world who would love to destroy the light.

The astrologers traveled far, guided by a star, to pay homage to the birth of a great light. These astrologers provide us with an image of awe and wonder as they capture the hopes and dreams of the world. This becomes our spiritual quest as well — to follow that star, no matter how hopeless our journey may seem at times; no matter how far we have yet to go to realize the dream. We who follow the star are filled with God's radiant light and keep alive these ancient hopes. Like the astrologers, when we are confronted with enemies of hope, we must look for alternate routes to avoid the darkness and walk in the light.

THE GIFTS WE BRING ON THE JOURNEY

One way we can do this is by identifying our very lives with the gifts of these three astrologers. They brought gifts of gold, frankincense and myrrh — simple gifts, but profound symbols that capture our relationship with this newborn king. The gold, of course, is fit for a king. This infant is a king who has come into this world with a gentle love and holy patience that will rule this world. The aroma of incense is sweet, and as we watch the smoke rise to the heavens we are reminded that Jesus is one with God. Though divine, he humbled himself, becoming one with us to show us how the dream of divinity becomes real.

And the myrrh, used to prepare the dead for burial in ancient times — remember how the women brought myrrh to the tomb of Jesus — reminds us of the humanity of Jesus. As the astrologers' story suggests, because there is so much death in our world, myrrh will never be in short supply. It will always be on sale because the demand is so great. Still, the gift suggests something even more important to us soul searchers and star gazers, namely, that no pain, no sorrow, no heartbreak will be foreign to this newborn king. He will feel the depths of our humanity. This myrrh is for one who will die, but in his death he will release us from the cold grip of sin.

The astrologers' following of the star is a journey that each one of us travels in our search for hope, for fulfillment, for life's meaning. Like the astrologers, we search for the source of the light. We can see the star, but rather than standing in place, gazing with awe at the light that brightens the night sky, we set off in search of the source.

This is the spiritual journey: not just looking up to the skies but keeping our wise eyes focused on the path that leads to the source. Along the way, we may lose our bearings and need to stop and ask for directions. And again, we need to be careful about whom we ask for guidance.

To find the truth of our own story, we must be like those astrologers: steadfast and focused, passionate in our purpose and perseverance, firm in our resolve to always be guided by the light. We realize it is the journey itself that made the astrologers wise men. It is our willingness to embark on the spiritual journey that will make us wise. The final proof of the astrologers' wisdom is found in the last scene of the story: Instead of returning to Herod to tell him what they found, they returned home by following another way. The story says that when we have encountered the source of light and been bathed in the radiance of God's glory, we take a different path home. When we hear and are present to our own stories and the stories of others written in the language of the soul, we begin to recognize the ways of light, we begin to align ourselves to the way the Spirit of light moves in our lives. We are changed by the light. We are transformed by the experience so that we allow the light not only to guide us but to fill us and spill out of us in our attitudes and our actions.

In the language of the soul, this becomes our passion on the road of transformation: to be filled with the light of God's love. This love is kindled by the fire of the Divine Spirit. Our stories are penetrated by tongues of fire that will burn down the fences that keep people apart; melt the barricades that keep people separated; burn away the barriers that keep people at a distance. This is a vision of an inclusive community revealed in the last book of the Scriptures, the Book of Revelation. This is what the puzzle will look like when it is complete: a holy city without limits where all peoples of every race and nation, culture and creed, language and way of life will live together in peace.

This is the vision that guides our journey on the trail of transformation as we seek to become passionate pilgrims of love and service in a world so often wounded by sin and division. When we hear this wake-up call in the rest stops of the soul, we are ready to live the language of the soul and allow it to become the language of love in our lives.

THE STORYTELLER'S SANCTUARY

Chapter Two

Silence is not the absence of sound but the absence of self.
           – Anthony de Mello

There is only one journey. Going inside yourself.
           – Rainer Maria Rilke

As we embark on this trail of transformation, it is important for us to have a sense of what we mean by "soul." I have an image of the soul as the basement of the house where I grew up as a child. It was my grandmother's house, and my family lived there until I was a senior in high school. It was an old house, and the basement always seemed dark and damp.

In the corner of the basement was a coal bin. I still have childhood memories of the coal truck dumping the coal into that bin. I remember the coal dust that seemed to cling to clothes and body. Dad's workbench was downstairs, and it was off limits. Mom's old washing machine was down there too. It wasn't off limits, but as I recall none of us ever got close to it except when it was our turn to give the dog a bath in the washtub next to it! Things we didn't use anymore were stashed in the basement, covered with coal dust.

As a child, the basement always felt like a scary place. When Mom asked one of us to get something for supper out of the freezer in the basement, we tried to get one another to do it. What if an escaped criminal had slipped in through the coal bin window and was hiding down there? Such fearful fantasies flooded our imaginations. When I went down to the basement, I would turn on all the lights, grab the hamburger and run up the narrow steps to the kitchen. Without looking up from the newspaper, Dad would ask, "Did you turn off the lights?"

Every now and then we need to go down to the basement where it is dark and damp. Here we learn how to dream in the depths of our experience. When we have the courage to go down to the soul, we discover our true selves. In the corners of our souls are those boxes filled with childhood toys, some covered with the dust of age and memory, that speak of innocence lost. In the corners of our souls are those snapshots of our family life — faces sometimes filled with smiles and sometimes stained with tears. In the corners of our souls are those memories of times we can't reclaim but must never forget.

The basement can sometimes seem a scary place; it can also be a place of refuge. What we hear in the darkness of the cellar we call the soul is the beating of our own hearts. When illness imprisons our body and brings us to the brink of despair; when friends turn away or fail to stay; when wounds welt on our memories and leave us bruised and bleeding; when tragedy topples us and death takes from us someone we love, the darkness will seem overwhelming and our hearts will skip a beat. If we listen closely, however, in between the beats of our broken hearts we will hear the whisper of God.

While we may find sanctuary in the cellar of our souls, there are no bargains in the basement, only truth. And silence. The cost for both truth and silence is steep. It is the price we pay when we realize that to be human is an attitude of the heart and the soul first; only then does it become an activity of the hands and feet. Before we can adopt a hands-on policy of meeting others in their need, we must first go downstairs to the basement and stoke the furnace of our own souls by sitting in silence. This is difficult because our culture places a premium on outward activity. "Workaholics" command more than a measure of respect, while those seemingly addicted to quiet or leisure are simply called "lazy." Our identity is often defined by our doing. When we are lost in activity, however, we tend to lose our focus.

Yet when we spend time in a quiet corner of the basement, we meet a God who desires our wholeness. We meet a God who also yearns for our unity and our peace among each other, who dares us to erase the barriers that keep us apart. If we take the poor ones with us into this soul basement, we realize that even though we may not be doing anything — like visiting the sick, comforting the afflicted, serving at the soup kitchen — the poor are visiting us in our silence. They are standing just outside that basement window with their eyes piercing our hearts. When we spend time in silence and see the look in their eyes, we will know their need even better than before. Then, surprisingly, we may realize we need them more than they need us. When that happens, our "hands-on" activity will flow from our "hearts-open" experience.

We need to live out this identity of being basement dwellers with tenderness and gentle compassion. Bruised hearts we will not break, and broken hearts we will not mend — at least not until we have allowed time for the pain to sink in deeper. Because we have spent our internship in that basement we call the soul, we will know that when the pain is unbearable, there's only one way to release it: go deeper. Get under the pain instead of trying to get over it.

In the basement we hold our pain as sacred. We refuse to believe in quick fixes but rather create an environment in our hearts where we can experience deeply the transforming power of God even in our pain. We learn to look at each other and our world from a different angle: from the inside out.

Because we have been to the basement, we know what our own dungeon is like. It is dark and damp and dangerous. There is a certain dampness even in the words God whispers. They cling to our memories like clothes caught in the rain cling to our body.

In the basement we call the soul, we discover who we are in memories from long ago. We blow off the soul-dust and see the sacred truth. That truth mingles like an ancient myth in our own experiences. It is the truth we learn when we walk in the dampness of our discontent and discover promise in the pain. It is the truth we find when we open the boxes stored in the basement, brush away the soul-dust and seize for a moment, and a lifetime, the stories that give meaning to our lives.

THE SEARCH FOR SOLITUDE

In this first rest stop for the soul, solitude is the antidote most often prescribed by spiritual healers for the poison of lethargy that so often seeps into our system. It can also be the remedy for the venom that sometimes flows in the veins of our family or community life: toxic sarcasm and acidic cynicism.

Every now and then we are obliged to find shelter in our own silence to enter again our own story. Then, when we emerge from this solitude, we will have even more truth about ourselves and more stories to tell those with whom we live.

As we begin this soulful search for our own deepest stories, we might look for that place, the storyteller's sanctuary, where we can go and learn the meaning of our own truth.

A myth that shapes this experience for me happened many years ago. The night was cold enough to convince me that this was not the best time to be alone in the woods. We had come to this place to watch a ritual: the Order of the Arrow. My older brother, Ed, was one of the scouts who was to be chosen to spend the night in the forest.

I remember the raging fire in the center of a circle of young men whose faces were illuminated by the blaze. For some of them, this would be the furnace of transformation from adolescence to adulthood. The fire showed the look on their faces — a mixture of anticipation and apprehension. This night they had entered the woods as boys. When the first traces of dawn would lead them out of the forest, however, they'd be men.

The one dressed in Native American garb danced around the circle chanting and singing. He was the high priest of the ritual who designated those few who were ready to walk alone. When his hand hit the chest of the chosen, it initiated the rite of passage. The force of the blow sent Ed backwards into the arms of his scoutmaster. This would be his only step backwards. From then on Ed would have to go forward into the unknown, the mysterious, the night.

Though this ritual occurred more than thirty years ago, its power endures on the fringes of my memory. It was a rite of passage that reflected those shadows that form deep in our souls which hold in their cloak the true meaning of our lives.

Every now and then we need to withdraw from the crowd, go to the forest and spend the night. This is a quest for solitary refinement. Certainly Jesus understood this kind of vision quest. In Matthew's Gospel, after a rather busy day of being part of a parade that welcomed him as a hero in Jerusalem and after turning a few tables in the temple precincts, he "went out of the city to Bethany and lodged there" (Matthew 21: 17). He spent the night in Bethany to relax, regroup and reflect on what was about to happen back in Jerusalem. Jesus also fasted: "In the morning, as he was returning to the city, he was hungry" (21: 18). Whether we escape to these solitary spaces to prepare ourselves for an important mission or to settle our souls after arduous activity, lonely places like forests at night and mountain peaks in the early morning light help ease the pain of our lives by forcing us to feel it more intensely. In these quiet places of the soul we embrace the heart of what it means to be human.

It is paradoxical, perhaps, to believe that the only way we can trace those bonds that connect us one to another is in solitude. However, as many pilgrims, from Moses to Merton, have showed us, solitude is a vital resource for the renewal of our sense of belonging. In solitude we face the stark and sacred questions, "Who am I?" and "To whom do I belong?" In solitude, in the dark forest or the damp basement, we learn the meaning of being human and holy.

Several years ago, after spending most of my life living with others, I asked to live alone. With the exception of one year of living by myself in Davenport, Iowa, I had always lived in community — under the same roof as others. I breathed the air of expectations (a variety of scents) living in community. I learned that living in close proximity with others does not guarantee community. At times I had lived *alone with others*. I knew what it was like. It was not community.

I asked to live alone for the sake of solitude. When I told a friend this, he said, "If it's solitude you want, you ought to live in community."

I asked to live alone not only to find myself but to find my community.

We all know how feelings get hurt in community and family life. Sometimes it's an innocent, or thoughtless, remark on the wrong day at the wrong time. Sometimes it's silence after sharing some good news. One is about to burst with excitement and seeks an affirming smile or a congratulatory word. "Share my joy, please!" is the scream from deep inside. But it goes unnoticed.

How often we miss each other when we are living under the same roof. How often the words come to mind when it's too late. I recall a brother who left my religious community some years ago. On the morning he left, a member with whom he had lived for years came up to him and told him how much this brother meant to him. "I wish you would have told me that before," the brother said. But the wound was too deep and the scar survived.

We don't do this on purpose or with malicious intent. Often the line, the joke, the words are meant to get a laugh, not to inflict injury. "Can't you see, this is the only way I know how to say I care about you? I make fun of you to show you I love you!"

Sometimes we are silent in the glow of another's accomplishment because we don't know what to say. We want to be sincere in our affirmation without sounding superficial. Perhaps we still believe that another's glory diminishes our own. Jealousy still hangs in the closet. We are frugal with our affirmation and greedy with our empathy.

The small house in the middle of the city where I lived alone for seven months was a gift from my community. With the gift, however, came a challenge, the challenge of silence.

Tony de Mello once wrote that "silence is not the absence of sound but the absence of self." Silence imposes a demand to search beneath the surface. Deeper. I turned on the television when the silence became more than I could hear. I walked swiftly by the door leading to my prayer room when the truth became more than I could bear. I escaped the house when the solitude illuminated a meaning too powerful to believe.

In the silence I learned this: It is safer to stay on the surface.

In the silence I heard this: Live and die in the company of friends. Laugh with them. Pray with them. But don't cry with them. It is too risky.

In the silence I heard this: Why did you join the community? Why do you stay?

In the silence I heard this: Where are you? Where will I find you?

And the silence resounded with even more questions: Where are your tears? Where are the shadows? Where is the night?

In the dark shadows of this rest stop of solitude, the storyteller's sanctuary, we touch the core truths of who we are: our limitations and our gifts, our fears and our faith. When we face into these truths that have shaped our lives, when we name them and claim them before God, we become transparent before God. We allow our Divine Parent to see through our fears to the faith that grows slowly but steadily inside of us. Gradually our eyes adjust to the darkness, and we begin to see dimly through the shadows to the light of faith that flickers like the flame of a candle caught in the winds of change. This small flame illuminates who we are in God's eyes. God is the Divine Parent who protects this flickering flame with gentle hands. And when we see who we are in God's eyes, we are able to see more clearly that spark of the divine in the eyes of others. By being willing to wrestle in the dark night of my own soul, trusting that God will protect this flame of faith, we are better equipped to be with another during his or her dark night. With gentle hands, we seek to protect the flame that flickers in the heart of the other.

HOLY GROUND

In the silence of the forest, by the stream or on the mountain, we discover not only who we are in relationship to God, a realization that will ultimately lead us to find who we are in relationship to one another (children of God), we also find our true vocation in life.

A Scripture story that reminds us of the power of discovering one's call in life is the story of Moses. On a journey across the desert, Moses is minding his own business while keeping an eye on his father-in-law's flock. Though he seems to be satisfied with his lot in life, remember that Moses is tending the flock because he is a fugitive. He had seen an Egyptian beating one of his people. Already filled with fury at the oppression his people were suffering, Moses kills the Egyptian and buries his body in the sand. The next day when he sees two of his own people fighting, he tries to break it up. One of them says, "Do you mean to kill me as you killed the Egyptian?" (Exodus 2: 14). Moses, fearful that his murderous deed from the day before is now known, flees for his life.

With the Pharaoh in hot pursuit, Moses goes to Midian where he encounters the seven daughters of Midian's priest trying to draw water from a well. They are being hassled by some shepherds, but Moses stands up for them and draws water for them. When the daughters return home, they tell their father the story of how Moses, whom they identify as an Egyptian, "delivered us out of the hand of the shepherds" (Exodus 2: 19). For this act of heroism, Moses is rewarded by the priest who gives him a place to stay, a job, and eventually one of his daughters in marriage.

This is the background that brings Moses to Horeb, God's mountain. It is here that Moses' solitude of spending long nights away from home tending the flock is shaken and his life changed forever. From delivering the daughters of Midian's high priest from the hands of shepherds, God asks Moses to deliver his people from the oppression of slavery in Egypt.

On this holy mountain, Moses experiences the presence of God in an awesome and somewhat terrifying way. Attracted to the remarkable sight of a bush on fire but not consumed in the flame, Moses inches closer. If we have ever experienced a night alone in the forest, we may know a bit of the fear that grips Moses when he hears a voice coming from the burning bush. It is the voice of God telling him to take off his sandals because the place where he is standing is holy ground. Moses' first instinct is to run and hide. He knows enough to realize that if this really is God speaking to him, he is in danger, for in his worldview no one can look upon the face of God and live. This seems reasonable. When we encounter the mystery of God in our lives, isn't our first inclination to look away? Moses, however, can't move. He can't run and he can't hide. Not here. Not on this holy ground. Not in this space of solitude. Though his knees are probably wobbly and weak, his feet are firmly planted, and now that God has Moses' attention, God tells him that the cries of Moses' people have reached God's ear and broken God's heart.

Exodus, a Communal Soul Story

The story says that God knows what we suffer and God responds. Moses' call to be prophet, political leader and even policeman for his peoples' pilgrimage to the promised land begins here on this holy ground. Moses is to become like the highway patrol for the peoples' journey to transformation. His staff will become the radar gun when the people are in too much of a hurry, going far beyond the divine speed limit on the highway in the desert. With Moses holding the radar gun, is it any wonder it will take the people more than forty years to reach the promised land?

Perhaps the reason Moses, the highway patrolman, tried to slow his pilgrims down and keep them off the fast track, had little to do with the fear of accidents. As we know from reading the book of Exodus, there were more than a few accidents, mishaps and crashes that plagued the pilgrim people on their desert road. Perhaps the reason Moses held the radar gun was simply to give the people time to embrace their new identity. Recently a history student at Kansas University told me of her visit to Russia. She related a conversation she had with an elderly Russian woman who told her of the difficulty the Russian people were experiencing in converting from communism to a free-market democracy. This wise elder compared her current situation to the forty years Moses and his people spent in the desert. It took two generations, the Russian woman said, for the people to replace their old identity as slaves and embrace their new identity as God's chosen people.

When we become frustrated by the slow pace of change in ourselves, our societal and ecclesial institutions, our families and our communities of faith, then our ancestors' experience of the Exodus provides a communal soul story to remind us that patience is a primary virtue for a pilgrim people. On our journey of transformation, we enter a time zone that is not our own. We walk within God's time, and in God's time zone the road sign says: "Speed kills." The journey takes time. In receiving his calling to be the patrolman for his peoples' journey on the highway to holiness, Moses would also have to change his identity. He would no longer be a fugitive running from the law but rather the lawgiver. First, however, he would have to return to the scene of the crime. The voice and vision of God that Moses received on the holy mountain would lead Moses back to the community from which he fled to release his people from slavery and lead them across the desert to the brink of the promised land.

DANGEROUS LIAISONS WITH GOD

Moses' encounter with God on the mountain offers some fascinating features which reflect our own dangerous liaisons with God in the stories of our lives. When God first appears to Moses in the burning bush and his voice is found in the flashing of flames, God presents his credentials by naming Abraham, Isaac and Jacob, three of Moses' revered elders and ancestors in faith, as descendants. This insight reminds us that when we seek the space of solitude, we take with us the traditions and values of the community that has formed us and shaped us into who we are. We cannot leave the stories and memories of our elders at the door of the forest or at the foot of the mountain. These are our creation stories, and they are part of our identity.

It is within the context of our communal identity that we seek to discover our personal call. We have a responsibility to ourselves and to the community to seek that vocation which is uniquely ours. This is the only reason why we go into the solitude of the soul: to discover who we are in relationship to those we love and are called to serve. We know that our own gifts will be of little use to others if we don't first embark on this journey of discovering our self-identity.

Remember though, that after listening to all that is conceived in the silence, we may be even more confused by God's selection process. "Why me?" Moses asks God. "Why are you asking me to be the one who leads the people out of slavery in Egypt?" Moses is asking God the basic question of identity: "Who am I?" Identity implies some kind of authority. Recall that when Moses tries to break up the fight between two of his kinsmen, one of them asks, "Who are you?" What right or what authority does Moses have to enter this fray? This question seems to haunt Moses, who now asks God the same question: "Who am I to lead the people out of Egypt?" People who are sure of themselves, who are clear about who they are, reflect an identity that gives them a measure of authority. Their presence seems to shout, "I know who I am," which, as we shall see, just happens to be God's name: "I AM."

Moses, however, isn't quite so sure of himself. He wants more proof of his own identity before he accepts this call to the highway patrol. By reminding Moses of his esteemed elders, Abraham, Isaac, and Jacob, God may be trying to assuage Moses' fear of accepting this call. Each of these names represent certain stories of which Moses would be familiar. These were the stories told to him when he was a boy. These were the heroes of his faith tradition. Now Moses would find his place in this honor roll, but only after he begins to sense and embrace his own identity and his role within this ancient tradition of God's story, a story that is always unfolding.

As frightening as the initial encounter with God, even more terrifying is the venture God has in store for the one who has taken the risk to discern his or her place in God's story. But God appeases this fear by reminding Moses of the promises God made to his ancestors. God's point is clear: No mere human is going to be able to accomplish what God is asking. The scope of the mission is beyond a mere mortal's limited view or limited capacities. It is God's promise whispered in the quiet of the evening or just before dawn that affords one the only courage that one will ever need.

Still, doubt creeps in the shadows. Is it really God who is asking me to do this, or is it my own desires that are driving me? Like Moses, we want to be sure. So, at the risk of knowing more than we want or perhaps should, we ask the ultimate question: "Who are you?" In his soulful conversation with God, Moses quotes the kinsman who asked Moses the same question when he was trying to break up the fight. With this question that once again ties identity to authority, Moses seems to cross the line. He asks God to give him a name he can tell the people.

Since there are no boundaries to the soul, God does not get angry or avoid Moses' inquiry. Instead, God pins God's monogram on Moses' memory. God's name is simple and sacred and easy to pronounce: "I AM WHO AM" (Exodus 3: 14).

At the same time, it is also sufficiently vague. In ancient times, knowing another's name implied some kind of power over that person. In a way, that's still true in our culture.

When I was student teaching in a large Catholic high school, I made a point of learning as many names of students as I could as quickly as I could. It paid off the first day I had lunch duty. Certain students thought that since I was such a rookie, they could be particularly rowdy. As I stood guard over the lunchroom, the student leading the group causing the most problems was not aware that I knew his name. Since I taught freshmen and he was a senior, he figured I wouldn't know who he was. However, when I called him by name, the noise stopped instantly. Confused, he looked at me and then whispered to the boy beside him, "How does he know who I am?"

As bold as Moses is to ask, God makes it very clear who is in charge of the lunchroom.

Notice too that God's name is in the present tense. God's name underscores God's promise: I am always present. I am always with you. Just as God promised Moses that God would not abandon the people, God's name reminds us that God is with us forever.

God's voice — whether it comes to us in a burning bush or the fiery eyes of those we love, whether it comes in the sighs of the lonely or the cries of the poor, in the laughter of children or the whisper of a friend — is calling forth from us a response: Be faithful to the vision I have for you.

It is important that we remember God's name not only when the journey seems easy but especially when the path seems impossible. We need to remember God's name when we are tired to death, disgusted and distraught, frustrated and fractured, broken and beaten. We need to remember God's name when evil seems victorious and violence seems overwhelming, when injustice seems to have the upper hand and anguish imprisons our souls. When sin becomes more than we can bear or when guilt overwhelms us, when mercy seems a distant mirage, remember God's name: "I AM." God's name is forever in the present tense.

SOLITUDE AND THE CRISIS OF IDENTITY

This story of the encounter between God and Moses gives focus to the question of identity. In the storyteller's sanctuary of solitude, the basic question that haunts us is, "Who am I?" Moses' encounter with God and his boldness in asking the Divine for a name, a credential, to give to the people raises the question of how we would introduce ourselves to God. In one sense, the question is irrelevant because we don't have to introduce ourselves to God — God already knows who we are. It takes on relevancy, however, when we think about how we introduce ourselves to one another. Think about what we do:

I AM Joe Nassal.

I AM a priest, a member of the Congregation of the Most Precious Blood.

I AM director at Shantivanam, the House of Prayer for the Archdiocese of Kansas City in Kansas.

I AM a father, mother, sister, brother, friend, factory worker, lawyer, doctor, farmer, pharmacist, companion, social worker, writer, artist, poet, Eucharistic minister, teacher, trombone player, bowler, baker, introvert, extravert, etc., etc.

Moses' encounter with God seems to imply that when one stands before God and God asks, "Who are you?" and I say, "I am the director at Shantivanam," God says, "Come back when you really know who you are."

We know who we are when we are able to drop the labels and cling to the only identification that matters in the long run: the beloved of God. We are God's beloved. This is the basis of our covenantal relationship with God. As Stephen Levine has pointed out, all the labels we use to describe ourselves only signify what we're afraid of losing when we die. When God tells Moses the divine identity is I AM, God has nothing to lose.

That's why God created us.

Hope Is Not Consumed

The courage nurtured in Moses while alone with God on the holy mountain swells in him through the rest of the journey. For example, in Exodus 32, Moses is characterized as the capable mediator between God and the Israelites. In fact, not only is Moses competent, he is very persuasive. In verses 11-14, Moses convinces God, who is in a rage because of the peoples' infidelity, to reconsider "consuming" the people in the furnace of righteous wrath. Moses' argument is simple: What will the Egyptians say about the Israelites' God? They will say their God leads them out of slavery only to destroy them in the desert.

Moses is not only very bold in telling God to repent, but he comes across as very calm and confident that his argument will win God over. Could it be that the encounter with the Divine One that Moses had in the high altitude of God's holy mountain brought him to a new depth of his soul where still waters soothe the savage fire of anger? Moses is the friend of God, a friendship begun in solitude when two hearts, one human and one divine, connected to bring hope to a suffering people. As a friend, Moses calms God down with human reason: "What will your enemies think if you do this?" One gets the impression from this passage, however, that God is listening not so much to reason as to the soul of a friend. After all, Moses has an investment here also. He has risked his life and livelihood to respond to God's dream for an entire nation.

Moses the mediator is seen as thinking of his people and not of himself. He declines God's offer to destroy the rest of the people while keeping Moses alive to start over from scratch with a new people. He appeals to Yahweh's standing among the other nations in convincing God to curb God's wrath.

Moses' brand of charismatic leadership can be a model for modern-day ministers of myth in today's exodus experiences. Totally dedicated to the will of God, it is not beyond Moses to argue with God, to shake an angry fist at God on behalf of the people he leads and serves. His focus is on God and the people entrusted to his care. What more important mission is there for one called to leadership than leading and protecting a motley band of misfit pilgrims through a strange land? To put up with infidelity and yet to always stand with them, never turning one's back on the people one is called to serve.

Remember, however, where such service started: in an intimate and awesome encounter with God in solitude. It was on the mountain while he was minding his own business that the fire in Moses' heart was ignited.

The story of Moses in the solitude of that holy mountain offers us an entry to the spacious room called hope. We are familiar with the rest of the story. Though Moses led the people from slavery and guided them across the desert, Moses himself never reached the promised land. He died before God's dream for the people was achieved. However, like the bush that was not consumed by the fire, his hope was not consumed by the frustrating realization that he would never see the promised land.

We learn this quality of hope when we seek those silent spaces in our lives. Then we are required to bring this quality of hope back to the community, or else our journey into solitude will be in vain.

In human terms, we might think God was terribly unfair not to allow Moses to see the dream planted in his heart on that mountain come to blossom in the promised land. But in divine terms, we catch a glimpse of a powerful image of our lives. Moses passed on his dream, his hope, his faith to the next generation. The hopes and dreams we have for ourselves, our community, our church, our world are given to us not that we will achieve them all in our lifetime but so they can be given to the next generation.

This quality of hope is discovered in the language of our experiences and in our reflections on the reality of our relationships.

MOSES' PARTING WORDS

In the book of Deuteronomy, Chapter 4, when Moses gathers the weary pilgrims for a final review before they enter the promised land, we hear how Moses' hope both in God and in the people he has led across the desert is not consumed. They are camped out the night before they are to cross the river and enter the destination of their dreams. They have to be excited. What a long haul it has been; what a strange and perilous trail they have walked. Their forty years in the desert have included more special effects than a Steven Spielberg film. They have escaped plagues of all kinds, late night escapes, the lack of provisions, hunger and thirst, frustrations at leadership, grumbling, adoring a golden calf and receiving a covenant written in stone. These experiences and more have defined the journey of these desert sojourners.

Beginning in the morning when they will cross the river, however, they will be nomads no longer. Now they will settle a new land — the land God promised them from the start. Now they have finally arrived. They are on the brink of their dream land — on the threshold of their transformation in the promised land.

However, before they step onto this land, Moses wants them to step back in time and retrace all the steps — large ones and small, missteps and stumblings — that have brought them here. Moses is reminding them of the stories. Don't forget the experiences that brought you here, the dying prophet tells his followers. Fix them in your heart. Fix in your heart that God is in the heavens and on the earth below. It is God who brought you to this point of great promise. Don't forget. Never forget that without God you would still be slaves. Without God you would still be singing psalms in a foreign land. Without God, you would not have survived this dangerous desert sojourn.

Moses warns the people that once they enter the promised land, the temptation will be to not rely on God anymore. Once they are settled on the land, it will be easy to be seduced into thinking that they have it made, that they don't need God. Moses tries to carve upon their memories the truth that even though they have at last found a home in this land, they can't forget the rules of the desert road. "You must keep God's statutes and commandments which I enjoin on you today," Moses tells them, "that you and your children may prosper, and that you may have long life on the land" (Deuteronomy 4: 40). This is Moses' dying wish, his parting words: "Don't forget the reality of God's relationship with you."

Moses reminds the people how God was with them throughout their journey and will be with them as they settle in their new land. This is the promise of relationship found in our personal stories — I will never leave you, I will never forsake you, I will never leave you orphaned. It is this promise that forms the foundation of fidelity in relationship. It is the reality of our relationships with God and with one another that makes our world a land of promise.

When we remember the relationship God desires with us, we live the mystery of hope. As in any relationship, there is mystery. What relationship in our lives doesn't contain some ambiguity? The mystery is not meant to be unraveled or solved but deepened. The desire to live in this relationship is what matters. Don't forget. How can we ever forget a friend who has protected and provided, rescued and reconciled, laughed and cried with us?

Solitude seeks to restore our remembrances of those relationships that reflect God's presence. It seeks to remind us that no matter where we settle or how often we move, it is the force of these relationships that stays with us. As God is a relationship of Mother/Father, Son and Spirit, so we are in relationship with God and with one another. The deeper the relationship, the wider the mystery.

BUMPING INTO GOD

From the stories that rise from the cellar of our souls, we fill the houses where we live with hope. As we remember these stories, we begin to see the image of God in ourselves and so are able recognize God's imperishable spirit in loved ones who crowd our living room. We behold God in the face of the stranger at our door or the poor out on our porch.

First, however, we must go to the cellar of the soul we call solitude, the storyteller's sanctuary. There we will find a story or two that will remind us of our own encounters with God and that will give us a larger heart when we leave the cellar or the forest or the mountaintop and return to our community.

Our quest for solitude invites us to focus our attention on God. Yet when we focus our gaze on God, we never lose sight of those who are in need. Once there was a pastor of a large suburban parish who often complained to his staff that he never had enough time to pray. So one day he announced that he was going away for a few days of retreat. Following the admonition of Jesus to his disciples, he was going to an out-of-the-way place to pray. He found a secluded spot in the midst of a great forest and pitched his tent. Soon after he arrived, he unrolled his prayer rug on a flat patch of ground and began to meditate. Sitting in silence for a few minutes, he was suddenly interrupted by the sound of someone running through the forest. He tried to focus on his breathing, hoping this centering exercise would help him distance the distraction, but the sound of the racing footsteps came ever closer until he was knocked off his rug by the person he had heard running. Picking himself off the ground, the priest saw that it was a woman who had charged into him. More than a little annoyed by this woman's rude intrusion into his space, he was about to angrily denounce her. But without a word of apology, the woman quickly got up and continued to run through the forest. So the priest brushed himself off, sat down on his prayer rug and tried to center himself again.

A half hour or so later, the priest opened his eyes and saw the woman standing before him. She was holding the hand of a child. "Sir," she said, "when I ran in to you earlier, I was in a state of panic. My child had wandered off while I slept, and when I awoke and discovered he had disappeared, I was so focused on finding him that I didn't even see you sitting here in the forest. I'm very sorry for bumping into you."

"That's quite all right," the priest said.

"May I ask what you were doing when I ran into you?" she asked.

"Why, I was praying," the priest said. "I was trying to focus all of my attention on God."

"You mean your were focusing all your attention on God the same way I was focusing all my attention on my lost child?" the woman asked.

"Yes, I guess you could say that."

"Well, then," the woman said, "I suppose no apology is necessary."

The priest looked at her with a puzzled look on his face. "What do you mean?"

The woman looked at her child and then at the priest. "Because you were so focused on God, just as I didn't notice you sitting here, you probably didn't notice me running into you."

Having said this, the woman and her child walked away. And the priest was left alone in that out-of-the-way place to ponder the woman's wise teaching about prayer.

When we take the risk to enter the rest stop of the soul, whether the rest stop is the basement where we check the sources that shape our lives or an out-of-the-way place for prayer and retreat, we might be knocked off course for a while by a tiny, whispering sound, or by the memory of grief, or by the exhilaration we feel for our family, our ministry or our friends. We may be knocked off our prayer rug when we focus all of our energy, all of our attention on God and notice how our prayer in the basement or an out-of-the-way place is not an escape from ourselves or others but rather an avenue for entering more deeply into the Divine Mystery that ultimately unites us all. It is in this holy communion at the rest stop we call the soul that we will learn the true meaning of transformation.

READING BETWEEN THE LINES

Chapter Three

Life is God's novel. Let God write it.
— Isaac Singer

The world is God's language to us.
— Simone Weil

We have established that the experience of conversion implies change. On the trail of transformation, we have to be open to being changed. As Moses' initial encounter with God on the holy mountain and his subsequent conversations with God during the desert sojourn show us, we are most vulnerable to the experience of transformation in solitude when we touch again the stories that shape our lives.

Once a friend was listening to my litany of lamentations regarding the slow pace of change I see in myself, in my community and in my church. I wanted to see, if not results, at least some evidence of progress. As I was talking, he reached for a book on the shelf and began flipping through the pages. He asked me if when I'm reading a book I go to the last chapter first to see how the story will end.

He made his point. This friend spends a lot of time in his own cellar blowing the dust off ancient manuscripts that contain the myths, the legends, the stories of his soul. On the trail of transformation, we take one page at a time and live the story. We turn the pages slowly and let go of the ending. We read between the lines and pay attention to the notes scratched in the margin because that's where we will find the handwriting of God.

Though we are tempted at times to skip to the last chapter to see how the story will end, the rest stops along the way teach us to try to savor the story, enjoy the characters and trust the twists and turns of the plot because we know the handwriting is not on the wall but in the soul. The manuscript for our future is in our hands. Nevertheless, it's wise to read between the lines and look to the margin because there we will discover our story is also in the hands of God, who just happens to be a very skillful editor.

Novelist Isaac Singer once said, "Life is God's novel. Let God write it." Our lives are open books in which God can write a new language of love on the pages of history. At the rest stops of the soul, we focus on what prolific and prophetic prose God has been writing in our lives. We become more aware of the poetic images of promise and pain that are etched upon our souls. In our prayer at the rest stops of the soul, we take time to see how God's great love for us is being played out on the pages of our lives.

From the Christian perspective, God's novel is about how God created the world and was incarnated in the person of Jesus in order to walk the trail of transformation with us, to show us the way and to redeem the world through his suffering, death and resurrection. Jesus is the new Moses who leads the human race in a measured pace across the wilderness of our world to a new promised land, a new creation, to new heavens and a new earth.

The story says that God became one of us to win our hearts and lives over to a new covenant of love. This story has been written again and again — from the lives of Abraham and Sarah, through Moses and Miriam, Joseph and Mary, to our own grandmothers and grandfathers. God's novel is being written again in our lives.

When others pick up the book of our lives, what do they read? What do our words, our lives, say about God's unending story of salvation?

SOUL: A SHOE SHINE SPIRITUALITY

Browsing through the newspaper one day, I noticed a large headline on the obituary page announcing that George D. Flanigan had died. I didn't know him, nor did I recognize the name. Still, I was intrigued by this man's death because of what he did for a living. You see, for more than thirty years, George Flanigan shined shoes on the corner of 10th and Olive Streets in downtown St. Louis. His death on Friday, December 9, 1994 at Deaconess Hospital in St. Louis at the age of eighty-eight would have gone unnoticed by most people except for his family and friends because George Flanigan was not famous. He did not make a name or a fortune for himself. He shined the shoes of judges and lawyers, doctors and business executives, people of stature and success who made tons more money than he did. But with the dollar bills he saved from shining shoes, George Flanigan put his son through medical school. From his perch on what many would consider the lowest rung on the ladder of success, George Flanigan not only made a living, he made a life for himself, his wife and his family. In the obituary, his son said this about his father, "He never met a stranger. He would tell people that even though he never finished school, he had a son who is a medical doctor and a grandson who is a medical doctor."

The simple but sacred life of shoe shine man George Flanigan reflects a spirituality that surfaces often in Scripture stories. For example, the life of George Flanigan, the shoe shine man, is similar to what the prophet Micah says about that little town of Bethlehem: "Too small to be among the clans of Judah, from you shall come forth from me one who is to be ruler in Israel" (Micah 5: 1). From this tiny, no-count, bump-in-the-road, blink-and-you'll-miss-it kind of town, comes the savior of the world.

The Scripture stories in God's novel remind us that we are never too small to count, never too little to matter, never too poor to be saved or to pass on to the next generation the riches of friendship, affection and commitment. The chapters in God's novel which chronicle the world's redemption tell us that when we are too small to think we can make much difference, the little town of Bethlehem becomes our beacon. When we think ourselves too little to let our voice be heard in the great conversations of our day, Bethlehem becomes our voice. When we think ourselves too poor to provide for others a place of shelter and safety, a barn in Bethlehem County becomes our refuge.

This abandoned manger in the boondocks on the outskirts of

Bethlehem becomes the place where the first chapters of a shoe shine spirituality are written. This is the place where people like George D. Flanigan find the story of salvation penned in the language of their lives.

LITTLE WOMEN

Two of the women who play a prominent role in God's saga of salvation, Mary and Elizabeth, provide detailed characterizations of why somebody like George D. Flanigan's simple life should be celebrated. Their lives were an open book in which God could write verses of victory on the pages of history. Mary and Elizabeth become major players in the second volume of God's novel, the Christian Scriptures, that tell of God's tender concern for the people of this world. This second volume of God's great masterpiece begins in unexpected places like Bethlehem and with unsuspecting people like Mary and Elizabeth who opened their hearts to God's great hope for the world.

Mary's cousin, Elizabeth, certainly understood feelings of inferiority. When Mary dropped in unannounced to help her around the house, she said, "Who am I that the mother of my Lord should come to me?" Well, Elizabeth, according to the recurring theme in God's novel, you are the perfect choice for divine intervention and visitation. After all, you are a barren old woman whose womb is suddenly, surprisingly, filled with a dancing baby boy. Elizabeth is the last person one would believe could conceive a child at her advanced age. And yet, here she is, full of life and being visited by Mary, whose visit causes her unborn son to do somersaults of sacred joy.

Could it be that Elizabeth's son, the one who would become the crusty and cantankerous prophet, John the Baptist, was already giving God's new novel rave reviews when he danced for joy in his mother's womb?

Mary, of course, is a prime example of such divine designs planted in the hearts of very human and holy people who need only say yes to God's dreams for the world. "Blessed is she who trusted God's words to her would be fulfilled" (Luke 1: 45).

Indeed, blessed are we who say yes to God's ambitious aspirations for us. Even though we may think we're too small, too old, too sick, too tired, too tentative, too fearful, too frustrated, maybe even too sinful for

God do to great things with our little lives, God's novel reminds us that the salvation story is written in a language only people from out-of-the-way places like Bethlehem can understand. In other words, the story of our salvation is written in between the lines of lives like yours and mine. It is etched in lives like that of George D. Flanigan and another shoe shine man named Sam.

A Shoe Shine Parable

Sam had shined shoes at the same corner for almost fifty years. But Sam hated his job. It wasn't the hot sun in the summer or the cold wind in the winter that bothered him so much. Even the furious roar of the nearby subway trains every fifteen minutes did not distract him. What Sam never got used to and the reason he hated his job was the way people looked upon a shoe shine man.

Most of Sam's customers knew him well. Or at least they knew his name and patronized his trade. "Another good job, Sammy," they would say as they flipped him a silver piece or placed a couple of bucks in his shirt pocket. The money didn't matter much to Sam. He lived simply on what he made from his shoe shine stand. The YMCA had good mattresses and Cal's Coffee Shop on the corner served good chili. No, what made Sam mourn his state in life was the way people looked down at him — or perhaps, more accurately, the way Sam looked down on himself.

One cold, blustery December afternoon, while Sam was shining a customer's shoes, a little girl appeared. She stood next to the space heater that Sam used to keep his customers and himself warm in his small shoe shine stand. The little girl kept staring at him until finally Sam did his best W.C. Fields' imitation and said, "Get away, kid, you bother me."

But the little girl stayed. "I've come to grant you a wish," she said. "Just name whatever you want, and I will grant it."

"A wish, huh?"

The man whose shoes Sam was shining looked up from his newspaper and asked, "Are you talking to me, Sam?"

"Naw, I'm talking to this little kid."

The man looked around. "What kid, Sammy?"

Sam looked up, but the child was gone. Thinking that the swig of whiskey he had taken for breakfast was playing tricks on his mind, Sam shrugged his shoulders, spit on the man's shoes and began buffing them with more than his usual vigor. A few moments later, Sam again heard the voice of the little girl. This time she was standing just behind him, whispering in his ear. "Any wish you want — and it will be yours."

Playing along with what he now thought was some prank being pulled by his friend Cal at the corner coffee shop, Sam said, "Okay, I wish I was the richest person on earth."

Immediately Sam found himself caught in a whirlwind. When he landed, he was in the most lavish house he could imagine. He was surrounded by servants who waited on his every word. Everywhere he looked, he saw money. Sam could have anything and everything he wanted. If he needed a new suit, he bought Brooks Brothers. If he desired another new car, he bought General Motors. If he wanted an ice cream cone and couldn't decide on a flavor, he bought Baskin-Robbins.

Sam enjoyed his wealth for a while but soon realized something was missing. So he summoned the little girl, whom he had kept on as an advisor. "Look, kid, I have all the money I want and can buy anything I desire," Sam said, "but the world just goes on whether or not I have anything to say about it. So you see, I want power — absolute control over everyone and everything in the world. I want to be the most powerful person on earth."

That was a pretty tall order. The little girl said she would have to check with her supervisor. But before the end of the day, the whole world was at Sam's command. His subjects called him King Samuel (you know how formal royalty can be), and he ruled the world. Nothing happened without King Samuel's permission. Wars were started at the nod of his head; peace was won at the wave of his arm. Now, not only did he have enormous wealth, he had absolute power. The world revolved around the wishes of the king.

One day King Samuel was walking through the streets of his empire when he heard beautiful singing coming from a church. The king told his entourage to wait outside, and he went in to see why the people were singing. He touched the arm of an old woman sitting in the back pew. At the sight of the king, the old woman trembled with fear. "What are all these people doing here?" the king asked her sharply.

"Why, your majesty," the old woman whispered, "they are praying."

"Praying?" King Samuel said. Then a slight smile creased his face. He realized they were probably praying to him, their king. But he wanted to hear the old woman say it. "And to whom are they praying?"

The old woman's eyes held a hint of surprise. She looked away from the king and traced the floor as she mumbled, "Why, to God, your majesty. They are praying to God."

The king could hardly believe his ears. "God?" he said in shock giving way quickly to rage. The king ran out of the church, stormed past his followers and went straight to the castle. He summoned the little girl.

"Look here, kid," King Samuel said in a loud, angry voice, "I thought you made me the most powerful person on earth. But my subjects are praying to one more powerful than I. So at the risk of losing your life, make me God."

"Are you sure?" the little girl asked.

"Of course I'm sure," the king shouted. "Make me as this God of the people would appear if he came to earth."

This time the little girl did not have to call her supervisor. She simply snapped her fingers and granted the king's request. Immediately Sam was back at his stand on the street corner, shining another customer's shoes.

What Others Are Reading

This story has been written again and again — from the prophet Micah's reference to that out-of-the-way place called Bethlehem; through two women, Mary and Elizabeth, one young and one old, who trusted that God's story was true; to an eighty-eight-year-old shoe shine man in St. Louis who lived to provide for his family, to give his son a future and to give all those his son would serve as a doctor a measure of healing and hope.

God's novel is being written again today in our lives. When others pick up the book of our lives, what do they read? Do they read a language of compromise and caution, a dialect of distance from others, a grammar of greed and consumption, and a rhetoric of suspicion toward those who are different? On the trail of transformation, we learn a new language of love and respect that transcends distinctions of color, creed and culture. This new language communicates reverence for those who are different from us. This language, heard in soulful conversations with both friend and foe, communicates compassion and creates communion. That is why in this new language of love there is no word like *excommunication*, for this word conveys the conviction that there can be no communication, no communion. The language of love discerned and learned in the presence of God's Spirit always seeks to keep the channels of communication open. There may be static on the line at times, but by listening for the Spirit whistling through the cracks of our sometimes broken hearts, we can keep the dialogue, the dream of reconciliation, alive. And, as my experience of taking Latin in high school taught me, learning a live language is always preferable to learning a dead one.

This language lives and is even more present in the absence of others. Maybe that's why, near the end of God's novel, Jesus ascended into heaven: to help us see that in the absence of the beloved we are able to speak certain truths that remain unspoken when the other is present. At the conclusion of Matthew's Gospel, Jesus has his valedictory speech prepared. Like Moses speaking with the people and reviewing the terms of God's covenant as they camped out the night before they entered the promised land, so Jesus is saying farewell to his friends. But unlike the people Moses was addressing, who were about to settle down after a long journey, the disciples to whom Jesus is speaking are about to embark on a remarkable adventure. Jesus reminds the disciples that as they set out into the world to proclaim the good news and baptize all nations in the name of the Father, the Son and the Holy Spirit, the blessing they give will be the sign that will accompany them: "Know that I am with you always, until the end of the world" (Matthew 28: 20).

These are the words, the promise, they are to etch upon their hearts in the absence of Jesus. It is this promise that forms the bridge between heaven and earth. It is this promise that gives them the courage to write the message of the new covenant in the language of their lives.

When I need to convey to another a certain truth I have discovered in my soul, I find it easier to write a letter rather than speak this truth in person. Sometimes the words I want to say in the presence of the other remain choked by a fear of self-disclosure. It is easier for me to write words of affirmation, affection and reconciliation than to speak them face to face. However, whether these words of love are written or spoken, it is the spirit of that promise that "I will be with you always" that gives them meaning, that gives them life, that gives them the power to speak to the soul of the beloved.

This new language of love becomes a kind of sign language of God that reflects the presence of the One who inspires and sends us as people committed to the path of holiness. At this rest stop of the soul we ask: What signs of love, of life, are we communicating with our lives? Who is it that needs to hear, either by letter or by voice, words of affirmation, of inspiration, of affection, of reconciliation? What do our words, our lives, say about God's unending story of salvation?

The Doors of Discernment

In reflecting on language and speech, on what words to say and when, the Sufi mystics advised silent prayer. Before any words are spoken, the Sufis taught that words must pass through three doors. The first door is marked *Truth*. So we ask in silence, "Are these words true?" If they are not, the words are left sitting outside the door. The second door is marked *Necessity*. So we ask in silence, "Are these words necessary?" If they are unnecessary, they're left to wait outside the door until they are needed. The third door is labelled *Kind*. Are these words kind, compassionate, loving? If they are not, the door closes and we remain silent.

This insight from the Sufi mystics offers us a practical way to view the process of discerning the handwriting of God on the trail of transformation. When our discernment concerns what words, if any, we might say in a given situation, such as discerning whom to hire for a job, we should pause. If we imagine the rest stops of the soul have three doors through which we must pass before we speak or write or decide, we may detect some noticeable progress in composing our life story — before we get to the last chapter.

A Scripture story that reflects this process of discernment concerns the disciples in the Acts of the Apostles. Faced with a vacancy in the company when Judas resigned, Peter says, "May another take his office" (Acts 1: 20). However, in order to find the right person for this office, as the Sufi mystics taught, the disciples' discernment must pass through three doors. Discernment is not a matter of choosing door number one, door number two or door number three in a game of "Let's Make a Deal with God." Rather it requires being willing to go through all three doors in order to enter the innermost office.

Door number one is marked *The Source*. This is the first door of discernment: Go back to the source. Peter stands up among the gathering and places their meeting in the context of Scripture. He recalls the passage that foretold Judas' destiny and why he cleaned out his office. Peter acknowledges that "he was one of our number and had been given a share in this ministry of ours" (Acts 1: 17). An important ministry at that: treasurer, keeper of the purse. However, there is no mention that the one chosen to replace Judas would need an accounting degree or have to be a good bookkeeper. Peter doesn't insist that the replacement possess the same financial acumen as Judas. After all, Matthew, a tax accountant, was still in the company.

Instead, Peter simply goes back to the source. He quotes a Scripture passage that reflects the effects of Judas' betrayal: "Let his encampment be desolate. May no one dwell on it" (v. 20). Peter, however, doesn't dwell on the betrayal but moves to the point of their gathering. Again citing the source, he says, "May another take his office" (v. 20).

In prayerful discernment, we're not concerned with bottom lines or even particular talents or skills we bring to an enterprise, at least not in the beginning. The starting point of discernment, the first door, suggests we begin with God's novel. For discernment to be true, we must start with the source, the Word of God.

That leads us to door number two. This door is marked *Being Present*. Peter points out the importance of being there: "One of those who was of our company while the Lord Jesus moved among us, from the baptism of John until the day he was taken from us, should be named as a witness with us to his resurrection" (vv. 21-22). Both candidates for this office of apostle were there with Jesus from the time of his baptismal bath in the Jordan to his ascending flight outside Jerusalem.

This is one of the key ingredients in discernment: You had to be there. We say this to people when trying to explain something that words just can't convey: You had to be there. Both job applicants, Matthias and Joseph, were there from the beginning. Oh, they probably fled as the others did on the night of Jesus' arrest. However, except for this fear-based lapse in their commitment, both these men remained in the company of the disciples throughout the time Jesus moved on the earth. This gave them the only credentials they needed. This is what earned them their advanced degree: They were there. Meeting this important criteria — being present with Jesus — made both Matthias and Joseph eligible for the office.

Perhaps this explains why Mary Magdalene, for example, was not listed among the candidates. She would have been my choice to fill the vacancy on the high court of apostles. After all, since she was the first witness to the resurrection, I would have thought she'd had the inside track. Yet maybe she wasn't there from the beginning. She didn't join the company until later in Jesus' ministry. According to tradition, she began following Jesus after he healed her. She wasn't there at the start. Of course, unlike most of the others, she was there at the end — the day he died on the cross. She certainly went through this door of discernment: She was present to Jesus when the chips were on the table. So, the only thing I can figure as to why she wasn't being considered for this office (besides the obvious assumption that women didn't get to vote) is that she wasn't there at the beginning.

Or, maybe more to the point, since she had brought the others the news that the tomb was empty, she was already the apostle to the apostles. So being one of the twelve would have been a demotion.

After passing through these first two doors of discernment, one reaches the third door. It is the door marked *Prayer*. This is the door that closes the deal. Peter prays, "O God, you read our hearts. Make known to us which of these two you choose for this apostolic ministry" (vv. 24-25). So they pray. They enter into silence. They listen. Only after they have spent time in silence, allowing God to read their hearts, scan the pages of their lives, make notes in the margins, edit a few errors; only when they have opened their hearts to allow God to read them like an open book, can they draw lots. Cast votes. Draw straws.

"The choice fell to Matthias" (v. 22) He becomes the twelfth apostle, filling out the unexpired term of Judas, who'd resigned from the company. He is the one who has passed through the three doors to enter the office reserved for an apostle.

This choice might have surprised the one recording this election process. After all, in listing the names of the candidates, he gives Joseph top billing. He also lists his nicknames. This implies that Joseph was better known than Matthias. We don't give nicknames to people we don't know well. This Joseph must have been well-known because he had two nicknames: Barsabbas and Justus. People with two or more nick-names probably hold some kind of status or recognition in the group.

This point underscores the meaning of true discernment: It's not what *we* know about a person but what God knows — and God chose Matthias. Sometimes God might surprise us. That's the danger of discernment. God reads our hearts. In the process of discernment, prayer makes our hearts an open book. When we open the book, God will open the door.

Allowing the wind of God's Spirit to turn the pages of our life stories is not easy. After all, when I read a good book, I often mark it up — write in the margins, highlight certain passages, underline and underscore certain words I want to remember. Maybe the process of discernment is about putting down the pen and yellow marker and simply opening the book — allowing the finger of God to peruse the passages, highlight the stories, turn the pages. When the prayer is complete and the book is closed, the door is blown open by the Spirit Wind.

If we are true to this discernment in the practice of our lives, we will learn not to be surprised by who or what may be standing behind door number three.

An Open Book

God knows us like an open book. To paraphrase the psalmist, God knows when we sit and when we stand. God knows us because, as Peter prayed, God reads our hearts. The Divine One is an avid reader. God reads between the lines to find the truth hidden in the passages of our lives. God keeps an eye on the margins where we scribble notes we want to remember. With a skilled hand, the Divine Editor underlines key phrases, highlights poetic paragraphs, revises run-on sentences, erases mistakes. More than anything, God desires to dwell in the pages of our life stories.

What more important legacy can there be than if someone we know, or someone we've touched, or someone we've taught, or someone we've listened to or cared for in some way picks up the good book filled with the poetry and prose of our lives, curls up close to a fire and reads again the story of God's gracious love?

REST STOP

STORIES OF CREATION, INCARNATION AND REDEMPTION

The great path has many gates,
Thousands of roads enter it.
When one passes through the gateless gate
One walks freely between
heaven and earth.

– Mamon Ekai (Zen monk)

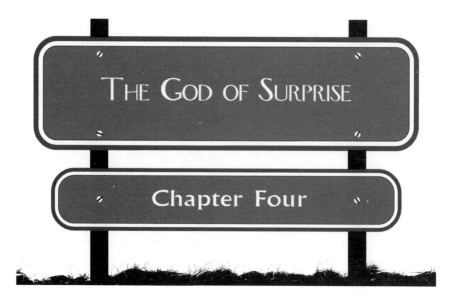

THE GOD OF SURPRISE

Chapter Four

You have seen what I did to the Egyptians, and how I bore you on eagles' wings and brought you to myself.

                                 – Exodus (19: 4)

If we don't offer ourselves to the unknown, our senses dull. Our world becomes small and we lose our sense of wonder. Our eyes don't lift to the horizon; our ears don't hear the sounds around us. The edge is off our experience, and we pass our days in a routine that is both comfortable and limiting. We wake up one day and find that we have lost our dreams in order to protect our days. Don't let yourself become one of these people.

   – Kent Nerburn, *Letters to My Son*, New World Library, 1994

God's novel contains three basic kinds of stories which serve as a map on the trail of transformation. We have already alluded to some of these stories of creation, incarnation and redemption contained in God's novel. Now we will look more closely at each of these categories as we trace how creation, incarnation and redemption stories fill the pages of our own lives. These are the stories we tell at the rest stops of the soul. These are the stories that reflect the various stages we have passed through on the journey of transformation. When we look at our own creation, incarnation and redemption stories under the light of God's *to* lamp, we will find our own truth — the poetic truth that will set us free enough to be transformed.

Our first set of soul stories that come into focus are our creation stories. These are the myths that remind us of where we have been. Creation stories help us touch again the beginning of our life's journey. They are stories that reawaken us to our life dreams and to the source of those dreams, a God of surprise.

PERSONAL CREATION MYTHS

Each of us has our own set of creation myths which have shaped our lives. Here is one of mine: A few years ago my dad was rummaging through some boxes in the basement when he came across some old photographs. What he discovered were snapshots and portraits of his parents, his sister and other family members taken when my father was a boy. The pictures are invaluable, especially the ones of his dad because he died when my dad was only four years old.

This was the first time I had seen what my paternal grandfather looked like. Now this faceless figure who died of tuberculosis when he was twenty-six — a man I had heard a few stories about over the years but who had lived only in the shadows of the past, this man whose name I claim, Joseph — now this man had more than a name. He had a face, a strangely familiar face. (At last I knew where I got my nose!)

I could see this man's hands rest gently upon my dad's youthful shoulders, large hands smothering small shoulders. They were hands calloused from working the land. These photographs, yellowed with age, awakened crystal memories that had been sleeping in my father's mind for years. These pictures spoke powerfully across the years with traces of truth about my family's roots. Like a miner gently chipping away the rock beneath the earth in search of his treasure, my dad retrieved bits and pieces of golden memories.

We tell these creation stories to see where we have been. We tell the stories of our ancestors to discover the richness of our past and so enrich our present with names, faces, events and experiences that will give some shape and sense of direction to our future.

It is necessary every now and then to pull out the old family albums, or that box of pictures or letters stashed in the back of the hall closet or hidden away in the corner of the basement, and spend some time remembering. Now, I know, there comes a time when we begin to make fun of these stories. Teenagers hear their fathers utter famous lines like, "Why, when I was a boy, I walked five miles to school every day, sometimes in a blizzard," and the response is, "Yeah, yeah, dad, now can I have the keys to the car?" Sometimes creation stories fuel only a sense of nostalgia rather than the sacred truth we need for our life's journey. However, when they are retrieved to teach a sacred truth, creation stories remind us of the faith struggles our ancestors endured. They call forth from us a measure of courage to face our own future. Above all, they tell us again that we stand on the shoulders of some remarkable people. We are here today because of the faith of our mothers and fathers. It is important to remind each other — and especially our children and grandchildren — who these people were. How they arrived at the place where they finally settled. What hardships they went through to get there. What their memories mean to us. The more we know these stories, the deeper we are in touch with these myths, the stronger our connections to our past and the more we will be able to sift through our present crises with the promise of possibility.

When we remember our creation stories, we rekindle the fire of our faith and give courage to the next generation. In telling these stories, these creation myths which form our foundation, we discover new possibilities.

The Danger of Creation Stories

In addition to new possibilities, there is danger inherent in our creation stories. For many of us the map of our memory is littered with creation stories that are somewhat like land mines — so watch your step! We want so much to forget certain experiences, to forgive certain people, to destroy the map to the land of our present pain. Some of us would like to go back and try this whole adventure we call life over again. Most of us would like to have taken a different turn now or then. Perhaps we hope that the dreams we had when we were younger would take root and flourish rather than die on the vine.

When our creation stories remind us of the promises and possibilities we once held that were never realized, we sense the danger of the stories. The greatest peril is to become like poets who have lost their passion. Consumed by loss over a life that once held great promise, we put down our pens and realize our blank stares cannot fill the empty page.

Take, for instance, the man I used to see when I visited a coffee shop in Kansas City. He looked the part of the poet: long strands of white hair hung carelessly over his collar. The lines on his face were jagged and deep as if they had been etched by a nervous hand holding a stylus. Countless crows had danced around his eyes.

When he was younger, he thought that by now wisdom would be his gift. He thought that his book of poetry would be read on college campuses and coffee shops. He saw fame and fortune accompanying him on his journey to the grave. But the muse left him long ago; she had been silent for some time now. His heart beat out of rhyme; the meter in his soul was strained.

He wandered aimlessly now, stopping here at the all-night diner to find his bearings. Cigarette smoke swirled around the stool, incensing his body, then disappearing, save for the odor that lingered in the air and clung to his clothes.

He saw an old acquaintance. She was sitting by herself in a booth near the back. A slight wave of recognition and a cautious smile were all he could give her as he tried to retrieve the memory of where they had met.

The chicken salad plate nourished his stomach, but his memory was still starved. Grandma's chicken dinners were not evoked in this cold dish of poultry and celery. It was not a distinguished item on the menu — there was no star in the margin. But it was the cheapest. He checked his pockets. Yes, there was enough change to cover the tip.

He lit his last cigarette and smoked slowly. Crumbling the package with his trembling hand, he saw the warning. On the napkin he scribbled his latest verse. It was not an original thought, maybe only an original sin: "Stopping smoking now greatly reduces the risk of heart disease." Or did it say, "Stopping smoking increases your chances for a longer life"?

It didn't matter, really. When the muse is muffled, one's heart is already diseased. When hope is gone, why look forward to a longer life?

FINDING NEW POSSIBILITIES IN THE PAIN

So how do we avoid the land mines of memories that cause us pain while still retrieving the promise of our creation stories? Again, we return to the source, God's novel, to find an example of a creation story from the biblical tradition that evokes the promise of new possibilities: the story of Abraham and Sarah. The story says that God selected a tired, old, sterile couple, gave them new names and the promise of generation after generation of children who would bear their names.

Tracing this creation story reminds us that the God of surprise lives. God's promise to this barren couple offers the kind of hope we hunger for today because for many in our world the present moment resembles a landfill — a land filled with broken promises and worn relationships that were tossed aside before recycling became a popular enterprise not only to save the environment but to save our souls. The promise God gave to Abraham and Sarah of a new land where they might settle and raise their family forever opens our eyes to a vision of new possibilities.

The story of Abraham and Sarah reminds us that chronological age is only one element of the equation. There is also such a thing as the age of one's heart, which cannot be fixed at a particular number. The renewal of our sense of the sacred begins with the belief that we are made to be "forever young." No matter what age we might be, God continues to call forth from us new hope.

When we are in touch with these creation myths, we discover in them a measure of courage that impacts our future. For example, when we think we are too old to start something new, we remember Abraham and Sarah. When we think we are too small to merit God's attention, we remember Bethlehem. When we think we are too young to feel the rush of the Spirit upon us, we remember David. In these stories, we tap our rich tradition. The challenge then becomes to translate the meaning of these myths into our lived experience.

STILL POINTS: SHAPED BY THE PAST

We are shaped by certain experiences in life we can never forget. Each of us has such moments in our own personal histories. Not only do we remember these events — whether they are sudden and terribly personal, like a suicide of someone we love, or occur over years and have global consequences, like our own or a loved one's involvement in a war — these events change our lives forever. Everything we do from that point on is somehow shaped by these still points — the points in life that years later move us to stillness and memory. They call us to stop and rest and listen to how our story is unfolding.

As we have mentioned, for our ancestors in faith such an event was their deliverance from slavery in Egypt and their subsequent walk on the wild side in the wilderness for forty years. Such an experience of deliverance shaped their relationship with God. At one point in the book of Exodus (19: 4), God said to Moses, "You have seen what I did to the Egyptians, and how I bore you on eagles' wings and brought you to myself." This was the still point, the turning point, in the history of a people. As they wandered in the desert, free from enslavement but unsure where they were going or how they were going to get there, God informed Moses that the Divine One desired to have a very intimate and eternal relationship with them. God called this people "my treasured possession." Even though "the whole earth" belongs to God, these were the people God chose to be "a priestly kingdom and a holy nation."

This Exodus event, which included the call to live in a covenantal relationship with God and the promise of a land where the people could live in peace and prosperity, shaped the life of the people. But as we know, the relationship between God and the chosen people had its ups and downs. At times it was difficult for the people to believe that God loved them so much. At times they grew hungry, thirsty, frustrated and fearful. At times they wanted to return to the slavery of Egypt because even though they were enslaved there, at least they had food in their bellies. They also knew their role, their identity. This new identity of being God's chosen ones, God's beloved, was just too much for them to hold at times. How can God love us so much?

It is in this sacred place of blessing, however, this understanding of God's love for us, that our identity as a priestly people is shaped. Without this belief in God's unconditional love for us rooted deep in our souls, our lives will lack meaning, our relationships will be shallow, our communities will be formed by convenience rather than commitment and our ministry will have a hollow ring. However we might image God — as Father, Mother, Creator — unless we experience this remarkable reality of God's gracious love for us, we will be unable to experience transformation.

There is nothing we have done to deserve this unconditional love. God's love is not based on an order of merit. The Israelites did nothing to deserve release from slavery in Egypt. Yet God called them "my treasured possession." This made the people God's own, possessed by God's love, compassion and care. Being so possessed, they are to allow this love to flow freely in their lives of loving service as a priestly people, a holy nation.

Christians believe this love connection between God and humanity is brought to earth in the person of Jesus. The compassion of God is embodied in the Son and the Son extends this connection to all people, but especially to those who are most in need of God's attention and affection. Isn't this how God's love connection works? Isn't that the truth of the Exodus experience that shaped the people into God's beloved? God chose an incarcerated, impoverished people without hope and brought them to a new land where they could serve God in freedom.

This creation story suggests that God's love is for all people but is known especially by those who most need to experience it. God's compassion for all the suffering the people experienced in Egypt moved God's heart to respond. Like an overprotective parent, God rescued them from the experience of desolation, isolation and despair. Then, however, like a parent who expects much of his children, God expected much from the people. God expected them to be "a priestly kingdom and a holy nation." They were to be a people who would give witness to the everlasting love of God for all the earth.

This is a remarkable responsibility entrusted to the people: to be holy as God is holy. No wonder they wanted to return to slavery where they were not responsible to live out such a demanding charge. However, it is precisely because of God's great love for the people that they were challenged to respond: to live in a covenantal relationship with God in such a way that God's love would become known throughout the earth.

The Exodus experience, based on the creation story of the first covenant God made with Abraham and Sarah, evoked the divine desire for intimacy with the chosen people. It is this intimacy that would shape them into a holy nation. But to become this holy nation, this chosen people, they would need to experience deeply, profoundly, God's love for them. Only then could they know that it was God's love filling them and spilling out of them to touch the lives of others. Their priestly mission, our priestly mission, finds its form, its shape, its purpose, its passion in this covenantal relationship with God.

THE MYTHS AND MEMORIES THAT SHAPE US

As we trace our own creation stories, this seems like a good time to ask ourselves what love has shaped our lives. Who are those people, what are those events that remain the still points in our ever-changing lives? Trace those moments when the promise of God's love became real because it was seen, felt, sensed in the love of another — a father, a mother, a sister, a brother, a community member, a friend. Savor those moments. Taste them again. Let the events, the experiences, continue to shape a commitment to be part of a priestly and holy people.

I once met a woman named Helen who came to the United States when she was thirty-one. Helen was born in Germany and raised in Russia. One morning I sat with her and listened to story after story of what she experienced living under Stalin and later, after she was shipped back to Germany, under Hitler. She gave me the tapes she made for her children which tell these stories. Helen knew that these myths must not be forgotten, but must be passed on from one generation to the next.

One such story involved the day Stalin's soldiers came and captured all the religious leaders of her village and the surrounding towns. The priests, rabbis and ministers were exiled to Siberia where they died slowly from starvation and exposure. For seven years, the people of her village were without a priest. All the churches were closed, stripped of their statues, altars and the Eucharist. They were turned into showplaces and dance halls.

So, under the cloak of darkness, the people of her village would gather in homes to pray the rosary. When a child was born in the village, the parents would bring the child to the community and sprinkle holy water on the infant. This was their baptism. When a friend or family member died, they could not hold public services, so they would gather in the home of the deceased and pray. They would reflect on Scripture and tell stories from the life of the one who was now dead. When a young couple from the village wanted to get married, they would witness the wedding. They celebrated the sacraments. They kept their faith and their hope alive. "It was the only way we survived," Helen told me.

This is the quality of hope that our creation myths seek to teach us. It is a tenacious hope. Tenacity is not often thought of in the context of hope, but the virtue is nothing more than optimism without it. Creation myths convey a hope that clings to a rope suspended between heaven and earth until hope begins to bleed. Tenacious hope is holding on for life even though one is so tired it would be easy to let go and let death win out. Hope is standing your ground when a group seeks to move you off your mark.

Tenacious hope is also tender: sprinkling water on a newborn child, comforting the old with warm hands; staying with someone who is dying and tracing the oil of blessing upon that one's forehead, celebrating the com-mitment of young lovers, grieving with the widow, welcoming the stranger. These are the meanings found in most creation myths, and they tell a tale we know to be true: Those who hope, live; those who don't, die.

We find hope in these stories of persons who have had the courage to face the truth of their own history. We find hope in the stories of those who have taken the time and toiled to trace the soul's archives to find a measure of meaning and memory. Being in touch with the personal and family experiences of sorrow that are part of each of our creation stories will give birth to new myths of redemption. Such myths will allow us to speak tenderly to those who hear only harsh words and hasty judgments. Creation myths motivate us to remember where we've been and why we are here.

STATUES IN THE ATTIC

In one of the tapes Helen gave me, she told the story of the time when many of her relatives and friends were sent to Siberia. Helen, her mother and two sisters escaped and boarded a train that was traveling to Germany. On the way, the tracks were hit by bombs. So they walked to a village where they begged for food and work. The people of this village welcomed them. They survived again because of their resilient faith and tenacious hope — and the hospitality of strangers.

Later, after she and others from her clan who survived the trials in Russia and Germany arrived in America and settled in the north, they created a Catholic community. They built a cathedral-like church on the open plains, the twin steeples rising to the heavens as monuments to the two virtues that sustained them, faith and hope. A few years after they settled, however, a group of Mennonites came to town and wished to make it their home as well. They wanted to build their own church, but the Catholics would not let them. This was their town, and the Mennonites were not welcome. So they settled a few miles down the road. Looking back at that experience, Helen said she had come to see how little her people had learned from their own experience of perse-cution. They had forgotten their own suffering and so failed to make the connection with one of their primary creation stories. This stop on their sojourn had failed to become a rest stop where they could sense the hand that had guided them.

When we forget where we have been, we are like statues standing in the shadows of the attic of St. Anselm's rectory. They were placed there when the church was renovated. To one visiting the attic for the first time and unaware of where the light switch is, the figures are startling to behold. Who are these personages lingering in the attic? At first glance, they seem like strangers, trespassers into this holy realm, but they don't move. They only stare into an eternal space, removed from the worship of the faithful folks who once knelt at their feet and prayed for their intercession.

Too many people in too many faith communities have become like these statues in the attic of St. Anselm's. We stare into sacred space but have lost our vision. Without a vision shaped by those stories of our past that give us a view into our present and our future, our churches become more like museums than sacred spaces of worship and wonder.

Once I was giving a parish retreat in a very small town on the prairie. The church held 700. There were seventy people left in the town. This church dominated the landscape. It rose from the prairie like a monument to another time, a time when the land was bountiful because the skies were generous. Three generations ago, this church was built on the backs of immigrant farmers who loved this new land and built this church as a sign of their gratitude. Now, however, it sits empty most of the week, and on Sundays the remnant sit scattered in pews owned by their grandparents, and pray for rain.

After Mass, one old gentleman who had long since retired from the land and moved into one of the six or seven houses that comprise the town said to me, "You didn't say anything about the church?"

So I told him I was impressed. And I was — in the sense that I am impressed when I walk through a museum and marvel at the art of the masters. As a historical landmark, this church has a place. But as a living sign of faith, well, the statues are in the attic.

The importance of these creation stories lies in living the memory. If we have amnesia about our ancestors' experiences of exodus and exile, it is much easier to turn away the stranger at our door or the refugee at our shore. But when we stop and reflect and tap the tradition of our ancestors' ever-increasing faith and tenacious hope, we find the courage to fashion for ourselves and our children a future.

Coming Home: A Communion of Saints

Creation stories awaken this communion of saints housed in our attics, saints both living and deceased. They bring to life again our personal and communal history, blessing and bounty. When we are willing to listen to each other's stories and are attentive to the pain of change that may be masked behind the stories of colorful characters from the past, we begin to realize that for many of our elders there are tears in the well behind the eyes that we call the soul. When we trust one another enough, the bucket goes down and brings these stories to the surface. It is important to drink from these wells of experience, to savor the stories of our grandfathers and grandmothers.

A few years ago at a "house meeting" at the province center of my religious community, one of the members mentioned that the steel windmill sitting in front of the main building looked "tacky." He felt it gave visitors to the center a negative impression of the place. Only then did the story behind the windmill come to the table. One of the brothers told us that the windmill was given to Brother Iggie by the students at our former seminary. Brother Iggie, one of the saints of our community who was renowned for his green thumb, for his remarkable ability to work with Mother Earth to produce beauty beyond our imagining, had this windmill amid his flower gardens at the old seminary.

Now the windmill took on a whole different meaning for the one who suggested it be moved. He thought it had been picked up at some garage sale somewhere; that it was somebody else's junk. Now that he knew the story behind it, he suggested we move it to an even more prominent place and get a plaque made that would briefly tell the story of Brother Iggie to visitors. Now the windmill not only told us which way the wind was blowing, it also reminded us of one of the saints of our community.

In the book of Sirach it says, "Now I will praise those godly people, our ancestors, each in his own time: these were godly men and women whose virtues have not been forgotten" (Sirach 44: 1, 10). Reflecting on the stories of our ancestors and the "windmill" symbols associated with them that bring them to mind and heart teaches us an important lesson about transformation. Granted, our memories are often selective;

we choose to recall only those aspects of a person's life that seem worthy of imitation. Though this can become romanticized to the extent that we might not even recognize the person, still there is value in recalling the "saintly" virtues of a person's life.

This feature of our faith, the communion of saints, evokes the power of memory and strengthens the bonds that transcend time and place. Saul Bellow once wrote that "there are stars whose light reaches the earth only after they themselves have disintegrated and are no more. And there are people whose scintillating memory lights the world after they have passed from it. These lights which shine in the darkest night are those which illumine for us the path."

Those people who shine like stars in the firmament of our personal history are the lights which guard our nights and guide our days as we walk this trail of transformation. These are the people whose pictures hang on the walls in our hearts; whose words are etched on our souls. In the words of the book of Sirach, though "their bodies are peacefully laid away, their names live on and on" (Sirach 44: 14).

Those who have died can be important mile markers on the trail of transformation. By remembering their lives and feeling their loss, by allowing the good we remember in them to teach us lessons in living with fidelity and friendship, we begin to sense the meaning of the ancient Native American prayer which reminds us that the Great Spirit has only "loaned us to each other" for a short while. When we remember this truth, the annoying little habits of those with whom we walk this transformation trail shrink into insignificance. Such recollection makes us more likely to treasure one another's beauty and not focus so much on how ugly we can be to one another at times.

By recalling those saints who have touched our lives with their grace and love, we are connected to a larger reality — one with all of creation, with all the cosmos and with all those stars that shine in the night sky. These are the stars that symbolize the fulfillment of God's promise to Abraham and Sarah, the promise of countless generations. These are the stars that will brighten the way for us when the road seems dark and dangerous. These are the stars that will show us the way because they've been this way before us.

Something else Saul Bellow wrote captures well this image of the communion of saints found in our creation stories: "Love is a power that can't let us alone. It can't because we owe our existence to acts of love performed before us, because love is a standing debt of the soul." Creation stories invite us to trace the memory and the meaning of those holy women and men whose bodies have passed before us but whose spirits continue to sustain us, whose love remains "a standing debt of the soul."

A MASTER STORYTELLER

This "standing debt of the soul" was brought home to me by one of the priests in my community with whom I lived for a short time. Father Kilian Dreiling was eighty-four years old and had been a missionary in my congregation for almost sixty years when we lived together. A few years ago he moved back to our retirement center in Ohio. The morning he left, I told him good-bye, and we promised that we would pray for each other. I extended my hand, but soon our arms were wrapped around each other in an awkward but emotional embrace of farewell.

I wondered that day if I would ever see Fr. Kilian again. A part of me believed that he went back to Ohio to die. The last month he lived at our center he often said, "It's time." Kilian had an impeccable sense of timing. In his preaching and the practice of his life, Kilian knew all the cues. For eighty-four years he had rehearsed this scene: "It's time."

Being a true missionary, mobility and flexibility were two of the charisms he lived by. His mobility brought him into contact with thousands of people through his preaching and retreat ministry. These friendships were not fleeting but survived over time and distance. The reason for this was Kilian's passion for the present moment. Because of his ability to be present to others in their pain and their promise, Kilian continued to bring others nearer to Christ.

His flexibility afforded him a resilient spirit. He was not a man who resisted or simply resigned himself to the changes that had occurred in the Catholic Church over the years. Instead, he tried to understand, ask questions, read and reflect, and so incorporate those changes into his life.

In the few months I lived with Kilian, I relished listening to his stories. One I remember vividly. It concerned his experience in the Pacific theater as a chaplain in World War II. After a brutal battle, Kilian recalled spending night and day anointing young soldiers dying in his arms. He prayed with them and held them close as they took their last breath. Hour after hour, he was present to these dying young men — until he finally collapsed from exhaustion. When he awoke, his pillow was the stomach of the last soldier he had anointed. Covered with blood, he went to the ocean to wash his hands, his body. When he saw the blood of these young men mingle with the waters of the ocean, he understood as never before the meaning of Baptism and Eucharist. Images of healing and eternity flashed in his mind. The blood of these soldiers, the blood of life, was now a part of the vast mystery of the ocean. This was one of the turning points in Kilian's life. Eternity touched time for him at that moment, and he was never the same again.

For me, Father Kilian was a modern-day Abraham. The only thing he resisted in his life was giving in gently to the power of death. Though his body was fragile the last years of his life, there was still fire in his bones. Though he had had most of his stomach removed because of cancer, the surgeons could not extinguish the fire in his belly. When he finally retired a few years ago and decided to move, he told me that he was going back to Ohio where many of our retired priests and brothers live to "light a fire under those old guys over there." I wished him God's speed in kindling the blaze.

Like Abraham and Sarah, Kilian was filled with a passion for life. Like John the Baptist, Kilian was a preacher with fire in his belly and fire in his bones. When he preached, this fire could warm the hearts of those who heard him or even scorch a few souls. Yet he truly lived the admonition of St. Francis of Assisi, "It is no use walking anywhere to preach unless our walking is our preaching."

We continued to exchange letters across the miles. A few weeks after he left, I received a letter from him in which he told me he was not in the house more than a few hours when people approached him to give a retreat. He was also summoned that day to the infirmary at the request of another priest who was dying. When Kilian walked into the room, the priest said, "Thank you, Jesus, you have answered my prayer. Now that Fr. Kilian is here, he will help me die." Kilian prayed with him for more than an hour and found a reason why he moved to Ohio: to help others make the journey from life to death to life again.

Kilian, one of the elders in my community, taught me to be available to the present moment by incorporating the stories of the past. When I am drenched by disappointment or never quenched by questions that have no answers, I draw some patience from the wisdom well of the stories of one of my grandfathers in community life, Kilian.

When our friendship was first forming, Kilian asked me one day if I would be willing to preach at his funeral. I told him I would be honored but hoped that it would be many years distant. Kilian died on December 7, 1996. The final page of the last chapter of Kilian's life story holds holy irony for this man who became a military chaplain in World War II: His death date was the anniversary of the bombing of Pearl Harbor. Irony would also dictate that I'd be unable to keep my promise to him to preach at his funeral. I was giving a parish retreat when Kilian died and was unable to get out of the commitment. I knew, however, that Kilian, a missionary who had preached hundreds of missions and retreats in his long career, would understand. Though I was unable to fulfill my promissory note to Kilian, I will always reverence the story of his life. It will always be "a standing debt in my soul."

COMMENCEMENT ADDRESS: LETTER TO A YOUNG PROPHET

The letters Father Kilian and I exchanged during the last few years of his life underscored how important it is to stop, rest and listen to the stories that shape us and make us who we are. These stories offer clues to life's most basic questions: Who am I? To whom do I belong? Why am I here? Answers to these questions seem elusive, but this should not surprise us. The reason why the journey of transformation raises more questions than it provides answers is found in the journey itself. A journey is a quest, the root word of "question," which in Latin means "to seek." If all of our questions had answers, the quest would end, the journey would be complete.

As these questions nip at our heels, wise travelers on the trail of transformation see these question marks as road signs along the way. Under these question marks, we stop and rest awhile. As we rest, we take from our knapsack some wisdom from the Chinese Scriptures, the *Tao te Ching*: "A good traveler has no fixed plans, and is not intent on arriving." This bit of wisdom is difficult to digest in a culture that places a premium on punctuality. Yet the wisdom of the *Tao* suggests that our destiny is found in the journey and not in the destination. The questions we encounter along the way remind us that we are seekers, not settlers. With this truth safely tucked into our knapsacks, the journey continues, the quest commences again.

This process of passing on wisdom from one generation to another is captured in such rites of passage as the graduation ritual. At this ceremony the students who are graduating hear a "commencement address." Notice it is not a "eulogy" that seeks to summarize this phase of a person's life. Rather it reflects the sense of "commencement," of beginning, of embarking on the journey once again. The commencement address acknowledges the wisdom gained through the experiences of this particular phase of one's life, but even moreso it characterizes the nature of the quest: that there are far more questions than answers.

Let's take a rest stop to look at one of the original commencement addresses. Imagine Abraham and Sarah about to say good-bye to their son, Isaac, born in their old age, who is about to leave home. The promise God had made to the couple began to unfold in the birth of Isaac, and he has been a dear gift to his parents.

So one night, Sarah sits down and writes Isaac a letter. She tells him the story of the night God called his father out of the house and told him to look up at the stars. God told Abraham that night that his descendants would be as numerous as those stars. Sarah reminds Isaac of the many nights they used to sit on the back porch and look up at the night sky. "Count the stars if you can," Abraham would tell his son, remembering what God had told him that night. Star gazing became a kind of game and favorite family pastime. In her letter, Sarah tells Isaac of her great love for him, of how proud she and Abe are of him. She says that no matter how far he may travel, he will always have a place in their hearts and their home. She says that no matter how accurate God might be concerning the number of descendants they would have, Isaac will always be the first fruit of her barren womb.

Sarah also writes about the hard times. She speaks of that terrifying moment when Isaac, then but a small boy, went camping one weekend with his father. That was the time God wanted to test Abraham's faith and told him to sacrifice his son to prove his love for God. They had talked often about that frightening experience and how Isaac almost lost his life on that holy mountain.

In her letter she recounts this creation story:

With sweating palms, Isaac, your father gathered the wood to build the fire, to slaughter you, his son. "Why God?" he asked, "This is our only son, the one Sarah and I have waited for so long, and now you want me to give him back? He's only begun to live. Sarah and I have barely scraped the surface of our affection for him. Is this what they mean when they say, 'God gives and God takes away?' But not my son, my beloved Isaac!

"I can't see it, God, but I will do as you say. I can't understand what good will come of this, but I will follow your will. I will sacrifice my son. I will give Isaac back to you. I will kill my son."

Drenched in sweat now, your father saw that the wood was ready. The spark ignited, the flames flashed and sent smoke to the dreary skies. "But, Dad," you asked, "where is the lamb to be sacrificed?"

Your father told you to lie down close to the fire to stay warm. He raised his knife and tried to avoid your eyes, but he couldn't. He saw terror in your eyes and fear in that face so young, so tender. He had never loved you as much as he did at that moment. His hand trembled even as his trust was growing that God must have something in mind here that his small heart could not see.

"Stop!" A voice shouted. An invisible hand held back your father's arm from delivering death to you, his beloved son. "Abraham," the voice whispered, "this was not to test your knowledge of me. This was to test your heart. You have passed this test of love. You have been willing to do the holy thing, which is, always and everywhere, what I, your God, desire. You have not understood, and you never will. Your mind will never know what this means. But your heart will. You trusted me. You would not keep your son from me. Though you have already tasted the bitterness of loss even before you struck a blow, you showed you loved me even more than you love this only son, this apple of your eye. Don't you see, old man, that my love for you is wider than the skies? And now, your love for me is deeper than the deepest human relationship, thicker than blood."

As you and your father walked home that evening, Isaac, after the ram caught in the bush was given to God in your place, you turned to your father and asked, "Dad, what was that all about?"

He tried to explain, but the words held no meaning for you, his beloved son. "Some day, Isaac," he said, "you will know. Some day, when you have children of your own, you will know."

You stopped and asked, "I'll know what, Dad?"

Your father looked at the sky just now turning to dusk. The stars were just beginning to blanket the earth. "You will know from what source your love for your children flows."

The two of you walked in silence until you reached home. I was waiting on the porch. Now the sky was full of stars. "I have never seen so many stars," I said. And then I asked, "How was your day?"

If we can imagine Abraham and Sarah writing such a letter to their young son and see it as a commencement address as he embarks on his life's journey, we visit the place where our creation stories hold the power to influence and to change our lives. It is the place where our older ones who have seen it all are still open to surprise, still wanting to learn, still believing that God is calling forth from them new dreams. It is the place where our younger ones who are eager and impatient for the future to happen are still open to listening to the stories of their elders and reverencing the traditions of their ancestors. It is the place, a rest stop of the soul, where we find in the holy exchange of stories new possibilities in the present routine and new hope for our common future.

After Isaac left home, I can imagine Abe and Sarah spending their summer evenings on the back porch, looking up at the stars. In the quiet of those nights, they marvel at the sparkle and clarity that lights up the sky. Even more, their hearts are illuminated by the promise God planted in what they thought was the wasteland of their lives. Believing in that promise, they discover uncommon peace in their old age.

Such is the picture I have of God. Sitting on the back porch in the cool of the evening, God looks out upon the universe. God looks at us children. Our names are inscribed on the palm of God's hand; our pictures are hanging over the mantel in God's living room. And now, what's left of this image depends on us. By taking the risk to enter each other's stories, we begin to fulfill God's dream for us — and so make God proud in God's old age.

The Importance of Rest Stop Rituals

Writing a letter to a granddaughter or grandson that contains some of the still points or turning points of a person's life is just one of the many rituals that are available to us at the rest stops of the soul where our creation stories surface. Other practical rituals already mentioned include recording these stories, as Helen did, for our children and grand-children; or, once a year, perhaps on the anniversary of a loved one's death, retrieving the scrapbooks and photo albums to remember the stories of our loved ones' lives.

In this age of new technology, video recorders and VCRs allow us to make a permanent record of our creation stories. A few years ago, I gathered all the old home movies my dad took of us growing up with his 8-millimeter camera and had them transferred to video cassettes. These old home movies had intriguing titles: *Uncle Pete's Backyard*, *Bob and Joe on a Pony, Joe Skunking Bob in Soccer* and *Look Out Below: Michigan Vacation 1963*. As I watched some of these family films, I remembered how my brother Ed, when he was going through electric shock therapy for his mental illness, would go down into the basement, get my dad's old Bell & Howell projector and watch these movies for hours, trying to retrieve memories wiped out by the treatments.

Such films remind us of who we have been and who we have loved. Such films tell the story of those we've loved and lost over the years. Such movies remind us of a time when hope was young and life not so complicated or cruel. Or so it seems now. Like those tape recordings Helen has made for her children and grandchildren, these movies have a common theme we must never forget: This is our life. For better or for worse, this is life.

Every now and then, my mom and dad show these films to their grandchildren to tell the story of what their parents and aunts and uncles were like as children. Granted, it can be embarrassing at times to see again some of the antics of our childhood, but like those pictures my dad found of my paternal grandfather, these films give the next generation some familiar faces and favorite stories upon which they can rely as their future unfolds.

Still another ritual that might prove meaningful is to visit the cemetery where our ancestors are buried. Particularly on the death anniversary of a loved one, stand at this loved one's grave and remember a story that stays with you and that has somehow shaped or influenced your life. Remember also that this will be your final rest stop, so consider what stories you are now creating with your life that those who come after you will tell to the next generation.

The rituals we celebrate at the rest stops of our souls help us to keep our creation stories in God's perspective, a God who continues to call us to conversion as we walk the trail of transformation.

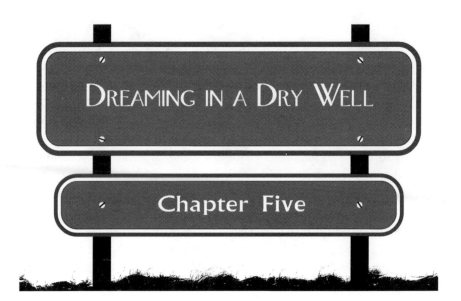

DREAMING IN A DRY WELL

Chapter Five

The mystery does not get clearer by repeating the questions.
Nor is it brought with going to amazing places.
Until you've kept your eyes and your wanting still
for fifty years you don't cross over from confusion.

— Jelaluddin Rumi

The best way out is through.

— Robert Frost

Reverencing and ritualizing our creation stories is essential if we are to move forward to becoming a new creation. The importance of these rituals lies in their ability to help us move on. This truth was sketched in my mind several years ago when my religious community sold the only major institution we ever owned, Precious Blood Seminary in Liberty, Missouri.

On moving day, many of us who were living in the area came to lend a hand with the move. As I look back now, twelve years later, I realize our failure to reverence and ritualize the stories of this "house." Our focus was on moving, not memories. I wish now that we had ritualized this loss of our large house. I wish we had taken the time to slowly walk through each of the rooms of that building with incense and holy water and told some of the stories of the people who had lived there.

I'd gone to high school in this place. We could have taken the time to walk slowly through the kitchen where the scent of Brother Carl's cooking would whet our appetite, and where our water fights while doing dishes would make us all wet, saturating our souls with memory. I wish we had gone to the classrooms and remembered the teachers who engaged our imaginations and stretched our minds. I wish we had spent some time in the chapel, where our prayer tried to stretch our hearts. I wish we had taken the time to go to the dorms, where the ritual of the upperclassmen "dumping beds" reminded the underclassmen that in a strange sort of way they belonged. I wish we had gone to the gym, where last-second shots were made and missed, symbolic of what happens so often in life.

There were many memories in that large house, but we were so focused on moving that the memories were lost. They were only to be found again in the years that followed when members explored their open wounds and wondered why we had ever made such a move. Without ritualizing our losses at the rest stops of our lives, we miss the opportunity to bring some closure to times of transition. When we fail to bring closure to our creation stories, we tend to see them only through the lens of nostalgia rather than seeing the sacred truth they offer us as we continue the journey.

As we reflect on the creation stories of our biblical tradition, our personal and communal history, part of the reality of telling these tales from the past is to teach us how to live in a time of endless transition. Some of us may be tired of being told we are in a transition period. We're likewise weary of hearing the old story about Adam and Eve when they were banished from the Garden of Eden. Legend has it that Adam turned to Eve and said, "I suppose this means we're entering a transition time."

Since most of us like to be secure and safe in our present existence and don't want to wrestle with the loose ends that hang like cobwebs in our collective consciousness, some of us need to return to our creation stories for refuge in our past experiences. These members of our families, small faith communities and churches yearn for the "good old days" and so tell these tales out of a sense of nostalgia. As comforting as this may be, there are other reasons to recall creation stories. The primary motivation for mining the truth in the stories of our past is to see how in a time of transition we often find ourselves standing on the threshold of transformation. When we find the truth in these creation stories and remember how our ancestors in faith survived in times of crisis, we discover more than a measure of meaning to confront the challenges of the present. We draw upon these stories to see how God is always drawing us, sometimes pulling us, through the transition to help us stand on the edge of a new creation.

The Sufi mystic and poet, Jelaluddin Rumi, offers some sage advice for living through this time of transition:

> The mystery does not get clearer by repeating the questions.
> Nor is it brought with going to amazing places.
> Until you've kept your eyes and your wanting still
> for fifty years you don't cross over from confusion.

A major temptation in times of transition is to pick up speed or push a little harder until we round the next bend. We do this because we believe that when we turn the next corner, life will be more settled, our vision a little clearer. We hold on to the hope that around the corner there will be a place where we can settle down and bring a little order to the chaos that transitions inevitably unleash. Rumi suggests that in times of transition confusion is a constant companion. The word *transition* itself implies being "in transit." We travelers on the road of transformation are by our very nature transients. This is a name most of us would not claim for ourselves since we now associate the term with people who are homeless in large urban areas. We would probably prefer to be called pilgrims or pioneers or adventurers or sojourners or maybe even tourists, but certainly not transients.

But in times of transition, we are transients rather than tourists, pilgrims rather than settlers. We make it through these transition times by following Rumi's road sign: *keeping our eyes and wanting still*. We keep our eyes focused on the road ahead while we quiet our desire to know what lies ahead. The creation stories we tell at the rest stops of the soul serve as a map to where we have been, the places from which we've come and the people who have walked these paths before us. We tell these stories not out a sense of nostalgia or a longing to return to the "good old days" — mindful that we are often selective about what was "good" about the "old days" — but because we want to keep these memories alive to nurture courage amid the confusion. Whether we cross the threshold of transformation in five, fifty or five hundred years is not our concern. Mystery always marks the map of the transient; confusion joins us for the long haul. Wherever we might be on the journey, the sooner we make friends with mystery and welcome confusion along for the ride, the more likely we will be to arrive at a place of contentment. In such a place as this, we will rest awhile to tell a story or two of how our ancestors of old made it through the dark night of chaos to the light of a new creation.

OUT OF THE CHAOS

The creation story that illustrates this pilgrim principle of living through times of transition is the primary creation tale from the Judeo-Christian tradition. Recently I heard an interesting take on the creation account in the book of Genesis. The speaker suggested that the reason God created the world was because God was lonely. God wanted and needed relationships, so out of the chaos God brought a sense of order. God created sky and sea, plants and animals, trees and flowers. God separated light from darkness. But still God wasn't satisfied. God wanted company with whom to sit on the porch in the garden in the quiet of the evening. So God made us.

This fascinating slant on the primary creation story gives us an insight into our own process of creativity as we live in those moments when confusion and chaos stake a claim on our lives. It is not good for us to be alone, God is quoted as saying in Genesis. Could it be that this insight comes from God's own experience of being alone? God is not meant to be alone. So God decides to live in each one of us and in all of creation, thereby insuring an experience of community for as long as God lives.

The Genesis story suggests that God is at God's most creative when God is alone, and maybe even a little bit lonely. The story reminds us that God's creativity was sparked by chaos. This is an important biblical principle to keep in mind when we are confronted with the confusion that presently reigns in our personal, social, communal, ecclesial and national experience.

When we trace this creation story from Genesis, we discover how

God's breath became a divine blast, a mighty wind, that separated the land from the sea. Then God inhaled, and when God exhaled again, the divine breath came forth in the form of a gentle kiss that brought life to the human. This is the heart of that primary creation story from the Judeo-Christian tradition that tells how the earth and human beings came into being. God's story suggests that the earth and each human being are to be reverenced and respected since the earth and earthlings have come into existence through the power of God's Spirit. The Genesis story affirms that, from the beginning of creation, human beings are God's beloved.

HIDE AND SEEK

However, we all know what happens. The time of transition begins when Adam and Eve are not content with who they are in relationship with God; they want to be God. So, because of their breach in the relationship with God by failing to obey God's command not to eat of the particular tree of knowledge in the garden, they are escorted to a new home outside the gates of Eden's garden. That transition continues even today.

We revisit this creation story of the fall by imagining God walking in the garden during the early evening. A gentle breeze is brushing the bushes and trees, the flowers and lush landscape. This scene is part of God's regular routine. God likes to take a walk right after supper. On these walks in the early evening breeze, God is accustomed to bumping into the man and woman God created to share this sacred space.

On this particular night, however, this couple called Adam and Eve are hiding. They hear the divine footsteps in the garden and hide in the bushes. In doing so, they invent the ancient ritual game of "hide and seek."

We've been playing that game with God ever since.

So God, the Divine Being, not yet familiar with this game of hide and seek created by the human beings — or playing along — asks the obvious question of Adam and Eve: "Where are you?"

Please note that it is God's question, not our question. Yet how often have we asked the same question of God? "Where are you?" In my fifteen years as a priest, I have heard that cry many times — from people whose hearts were broken; whose hope had evaporated in the burning heat of anguish and adversity, people who wondered where God was. Where had God gone? They whispered to me, "Where is God?"

Haven't we all, at one time or another in our lives, when the pain has become intense, when the loss has become so immense, when the suffering has been more than we could bear, haven't we sensed that question forming deep in our souls and coming forth like a sigh: "Where are you?"

We go looking for God as if God has finally learned how to play the game of hide and seek. Except now God is the one who is hiding and we are the ones who are seeking. We run off in search of God's hiding place. When we do, we fail to see that the answer to the question "Where are you?" is right before our eyes:

God is walking in the garden in the cool of an evening.

God is playing with our children in the backyard.

God is sitting with a dying friend in the hospital.

God is walking along an inner city street picking up pieces of broken glass.

God is hanging out on the corner.

God is sitting down for supper in the suburbs.

God is putting in late hours behind a desk or working overtime on a factory assembly line or out in a field trying to get the crops in before the storm comes.

God is sitting in silence on a prayer rug, or sitting in the living room curled up with a good book, or sitting on the porch sipping ice tea and swapping stories with a neighbor, or sitting in the back of a darkened church, long after everyone else has gone home, counting God's losses.

We ask of God, "Where are you?" And the answer is: God is in the routine and the remarkable, in the anguish and the joy. God is in the details and in the dramatic, in the brush strokes of another's hand wiping a tear from a friend's eyes and in the broad strokes of the red sky at dusk.

Yet still we ask, when the push of pain becomes a shove of suffering: "Where are you?"

And God replies, "I asked you first!"

It is, after all, God's question not ours.

A Hiding Place

The creation story of the fall raises the question: Where are we? The story from Genesis says Adam was hiding because he was naked. He hid himself because he was ashamed. Because of his shame, he did what many of us do — he looked for someone to blame.

Where are we? Do we stand exposed because of our insistence in pointing fingers rather than taking responsibility for our actions?

Do we stand ashamed because of the blame we have passed around to others? It's not my fault, we say. "She made me do it. The serpent made me do it. Why, God, you made me do it because 'the woman whom you put here with me, she gave me fruit from the tree.'" Yes, if we trace the roots of the tree of blame we can find the divine fault line in all our failures.

When we've run out of people to blame, we can always blame God.

But of course, our hiding place doesn't conceal us from God. That's what Adam and Eve discovered: In the very attempt to conceal themselves from God they reveal themselves. God knew that something was wrong. Something was terribly wrong. Adam and Eve were in hiding. Something in God's garden had gone awry.

And the shaming starts. And the blaming begins.

Where are we?

There are certain events in our lives in which we know precisely where we were when the event happened. The Kennedy assassination is an obvious example for many of us. Or, more recently, the bombing in Oklahoma City or perhaps the deaths of Princess Diana or Mother Teresa. We know precisely where we were when we heard the news.

Yet when chaos and confusion crowd our lives, we play this endless game of hide and seek. When trapped in turmoil or imprisoned by pain, we keep seeking divine assistance, but it seems that God is hiding somewhere in the garden of good and evil.

We keep looking for God in the realm of reason and logic as we try to find some reasonable explanation for why we are caught in this confusion, experiencing this chaos, undergoing this painful period of our lives that threatens to hold us under for good. And maybe in moments of divine illumination we do sense that this is "for our own good." Still, we want some reasonable explanation.

God, however, is rarely found in reasonable explanations. God is not often discovered in theological dissertations. God is found in walking in the garden in the early evening. God is felt in the cool breeze that brushes lightly across a tear-stained face. God is touched in the hands of another who is willing to suspend reason and extend compassion. God is in the one who is willing to stand where we stand, to be where we are.

So, where are we? And what do we see from where we stand?

SEEING FROM WHERE WE STAND

The creation story of Adam and Eve is a story of how we as human beings began to see with our own eyes rather than with divine eyes. God has been trying to correct our vision ever since. It is a vision that, in Paul's words, "fixes our gaze on what is unseen" (2 Corinthians 4: 8). We usually focus only on what we can see. "What is seen," Paul writes, "is transitory; what is not seen lasts forever" (2 Corinthians 4: 18).

What do we see from where we are?

Do we see from the inside out? Or are we on the outside looking in? In the language of the soul, those who live from the inside out know where they are.

Maybe this is the question we should ask of ourselves, of each other, from now on. Instead of that question we often use to greet another, "How are you today?" maybe we should ask of one another, "Where are you today?" Maybe that is the question that gets to the heart of who we are. Not how, but where. God knows how. Notice that God doesn't ask Adam and Eve, "How are you tonight?" God asks, "Where are you?"

God knows how.

God wants to know where.

Are we on the inside or the outside? Are we living from the center or crying out from the fringe? Are we hiding because of our shame or pointing fingers in another's direction to deflect attention and designate blame?

Where are we? Where are we on this trail of transformation? It is a question that will be frequently asked of us as we travel along the way. At each rest stop of the soul, God wants to know: "Where are we?"

The question reflects a sense of place. Where are we today? Are we in hiding? Are we lost in memory? Are we waiting to be found? Are we in a place called hope or a place where our lack of care feeds another's despair?

Where are we?

Are we in a good place? A safe place? A holy place? Or a hiding place?

God knows how. God knows how we got to this place. Now God wants to know where. Where are we?

So, instead of asking those we meet at the rest stop the familiar question, "How are you?" let's start asking each other, "Where are you?" Then, instead of moving on quickly before the other has a chance to explain his or her location, we can stand in that place with the other. Just stand there. And let the truth be exposed. The naked truth.

At this rest stop of the soul, we can hear God calling to us: "Come out, come out, wherever you are." The creation story of the fall of Adam and Eve that initiated this endless time of transition invites us to come out of our hiding places and see that we are willing to confront the chaos and confusion of our lives rather than running away. We are invited to see that we are in a good place, a sane place, a saving place. A place where we will hear God say, "Ali, Ali, in free."

The primary creation story from the Judeo-Christian tradition suggests that living in chaos is not necessarily a bad place to live. In fact, it may provide us with a forwarding address for the future. If God is most creative in God's moments of loneliness and darkness, if God created order out of the chaos and if we rely on God's inspiration, we might just find that we are most creative in those moments when we are most confused.

Rest Stop: In a Dry Well

As we look ahead to the trail of transformation that stretches before us in this vast landscape of life, one of our creation stories reminds us that we will come to a well where we will stop and rest awhile. We imagine this well will afford us a cool drink to refresh our thirst. But the well is dry.

Then, suddenly, when we least expect it, we find ourselves at the bottom of this dry well. Have we been pushed into this well? Like Joseph, "the master dreamer," have we been thrown into the well by people we trusted with our lives? Or is it that leaning over this well, peering into its depths, we simply lost our balance, leaned too far and fell into this dry well?

Does it matter how we got here? I suppose it does. Of course it does. For now, however, just sit in this well and notice it is dark but not damp. No water has filled this well for some time. Let's rest here for a while to catch our breath after the fall, or after the push, or after being thrown for a loop. Sitting in this well for a while, we may discover how this experience of being a well-sitter will help us catch God's dreams for us.

This is the dry, not-so-safe place where all dreamers, all poets and all prophets must go from time to time. Some describe it as the well of loneliness. For others it's the dark night of the soul. Still others might capture it in terms of solitude. Joseph, the master dreamer, spent time here. In a sense, so did Jesus, who was "the stone rejected by the builders," dropped like a rock to the bottom of a well.

Joseph found the cistern "empty and dry." At least he was still alive. Most of his brothers wanted to kill him and throw his dead body into the well. "Then we shall see what comes of his dreams." However, Reuben, Joseph's brother, spared his life and suggested a compromise to the cruelty planned by the other brothers. They threw him into the well alive. Such is the way with com*promises*: there is still some *promise* left when one spends time in the well alive, even when it seems one is left for dead.

Still, we might ask, "What becomes of Joseph's dreams now that he is sitting in the bottom of the well?" Perhaps in these close quarters, this dark cell, this deep well, his dreams had room to breathe. Or maybe more accurately, God's dreams for Joseph had some space to be clarified and cleansed. In the solitary confinement of that dry well, Joseph's dreams were refined.

This creation story says that our dreams need to be dry-cleaned in a dry well now and then. In this well, we are powerless and not in control. We face the "dry," stark reality of the darkness; our dreams are cleansed of illusion. When we spend time in a dry well, God's dreams for us, God's divine plans and not our illusory plans, come to the surface.

In this dry well, we begin to see what becomes of God's dreams for us — and what becomes of our own. For you see, God's dreams for us are our own deepest dreams; only God's dreams for us are worthy of being realized. Our other dreams — especially those meant to promote ourselves or gain a measure of fame or even a sense of security — leave us tilting at windmills.

That phrase, "tilting at windmills," became part of our language of conversion through another legendary master dreamer, Don Quixote. In Miguel de Cervantes' novel, the daring dreamer sits in a prison cell — not unlike a well — and spins a tale to his comrades about his fantastic adventures. One of these flights of fantasy concerns how he attacked a windmill because he thought it was a giant. Don Quixote's dreams had become delusions.

So will ours unless we sit in a dry well now and then and allow God's Spirit to dry-clean our dreams for the future.

We know how oftentimes dreamers are branded as idealists and ostracized by society and institutions bent on preserving the status quo. Those who remain faithful to the dreams given to them by God, however, often are called to rest in this well. The creation story of Joseph, the master dreamer, a foreshadowing of the incarnation story of Jesus, the divine dreamer, reminds us that sometimes we must be willing to fall into a well for the sake of our dreams. The world will be better because we have held fast to God's dreams for us and allowed God to refine and refresh our dreams. Though our dreams may receive the scorn of others and our souls become sketched with scars for holding onto our dreams, sitting in these wells will afford us time to regain our strength and gather the courage to continue the journey of transformation.

Resting in a dry well will allow us the opportunity to remember what happens to dreamers like Joseph and Jesus. Only by remembering that the one in the well who is then sold into slavery will become the symbol of liberation for his people, only by remembering that the one rejected by the builders will become the cornerstone of the new creation and only by remembering how important it is to sit in our own wells now and then will we remain faithful to this quest.

And only when we remain faithful shall we see what comes of these dreams.

WISHING WELLS

One day a few years ago when I was going through one of those periodic dry spells in my life, I was walking in the woods and came upon an abandoned well. So I pulled a penny from my pocket and made a wish. Even with inflation the cost is the same as it always has been: a penny for one's thoughts, a penny for one's dreams, a penny for a wish or a prayer. I wished I had had a bucket with me that day. I would have lowered the bucket down that well and maybe found some redemption.

Since I didn't have a bucket, I sat down with my back against the well and wrote this prayer:

Fountain of life,
stream of mercy,
send a river of love into this dry,
parched heart land.
Let your compassion creep and seep
into the cracks of my sun-baked soul.
This ground of my being is so hard.
It has been without water much too long.
Is this what they mean by burnout?
I was on fire, once upon a time.
Now I thirst,
wishing it would rain.

When we come upon those wishing wells or praying wells on our journey of faith, we should always carry a bucket. Lowering those buckets into the wellsprings of love, we would draw enough water to quench even the thirstiest soul.

There's even more, however. When I shared this image with a friend, he said, "Joe, you think the problem is that the well of God's providence is too deep. That's not the problem. The problem is, your bucket is too small!"

Thus, our challenge is not only to carry a bucket with us on our visits to God's well; our challenge is to bring big buckets to the well — and large hearts. For the well of God's will is deep, and our buckets are too small to carry the water of life we draw from this wellspring of love.

When we gather around the wells of our common life, we bring to these rest stops tales of our anguish and anecdotes of our desire. We send the bucket down into the well of our very human hearts to draw some hope for the journey. When we drink in these stories of wonder and of woe found at the bottom of each other's wells, we quench our thirst on God.

Our creation stories thus hold an inclusive vision. It is a vision in which all are included and no one is left out to fend for herself or himself. It is a movement of faith that is gentle but so effective. We are drawn into a circle of community, and then because of the story of our encounter with the one at the well we go forth to widen the circle of that community.

We are invited to drink often from these new wells of our God experiences, to fill our wells not with wishes but with the life-giving wisdom of our own faith stories.

DIG WELLS, DON'T BUILD WALLS

We have more than enough people in our communities, our church and our world today who want to build walls to keep others out — out of our country, out of our places of worship, out of our neighborhoods, out of our hearts. Walls only keep us apart, separate and distant from one another.

But the prophetic dimension of our desire for transformation invites us to be well diggers, not wall builders. By digging wells, we go deep into the soil of our own God experiences and find our common ground.

When we first attempt to dig these new wells, we may encounter some heavy rocks that will not yield. If so, remember Moses. Remember the creation story of how he was about to be stoned by his disgruntled pack of impatient pilgrims. But instead of being stoned, he struck a rock, and water flowed. As we have already seen, there are many times during our journey when we resemble our ancestors in faith. We wander aimlessly, or so it seems, in a parched, dry wasteland. Personal problems, tragedies and terrors of every sort stop us in our tracks and cause us to scream: "Take us back, Moses! What have you done? Have you brought us out here to die of thirst?" All of us are parched at times, grovelling and grumbling in the arid desert air. But then the rock is struck, and water flows.

And when water flows on dry ground, hope grows.

When we dig deeper into the wells of our souls, we discover a fresh water supply that drenches our bodies and quenches our thirsty souls.

The wells we dig in the soil of our souls can also become important gathering places around which we tell the stories. On a visit to Guatemala a few years ago, the women in the village where I was staying would gather each morning at a large well on the edge of the village. There they would wash clothes and tell stories. Many were mothers who had lost children, and women whose loved ones had disappeared during the never-ending night of oppression and injustice.

St. Bernard of Clairvaeux once observed, "Everyone has to drink from his or her own well." The women at that well in Guatemala were drinking from the well of their own experience of suffering and pain. But what was amazing to me was how their lives brimmed with hope. Even amid the pain and suffering they were experiencing daily — with friends and family members disappearing, poverty beyond description, injustice beyond imagination — still they believed in the one who stops by the well and brings life. Moreover, these women shared their faith with the unbeliever in me. They shared their hope with the desperate and despairing part of me. They shared their love and so broke down the barriers of culture and language that easily could have kept us apart.

Later, we traveled up into the mountains where some of our priests lived and worked among the Quiche peoples. The Quiche have a deep reverence for all creation. Earth takes on a sacredness, and they hold to an abiding belief that God has a way of ordering the universe in a very gentle way. There is not a word in Quiche-Mayan culture for "eternal life" since they live a kind of circle spirituality, believing that eternity is ongoing. Indeed, Guatemala is known as the "land of eternal spring" because of its lush verdant landscape.

After Mass in one village we went to take a closer look at a waterfall that cascaded down the side of a mountain. We walked a trail and found a pool, blue and clear, formed by the rushing waters. Here we sat to rest awhile. We sat in silence and listened to the roar of the waters. Later, we walked higher up the mountain. When we finally reached the place just below the falls, I had a sense of what baptism means: the power, raw and real, of water rushing down the side of a mountain and making everything it touches green and new. We were showered by the waters crashing on the rocks; we were drenched by water made holy in the stream of life.

The rushing waters of redemption reminded us of life in the midst of death. There is so much poverty and pain, so much suffering and injustice in Guatemala, but this holy place seemed to mirror the hope that we discovered in the lives and eyes, hearts and minds of the people we met — like those women at the well. Though accustomed to terror and violence, still they affirmed life.

They seemed to know that the problem is not that the well of God's providence is too deep, but rather that our buckets are too small.

A Gathering of Waters

When we gather the waters of our own experiences at the rest stops of the soul, there is a caution we might keep in mind. Though I believe we all are poets of our own truth, some in the group are more articulate than others. Sometimes we allow only those who are articulate, who are good storytellers, who can put together lyrical sentences and poetic phrases to dominate the conversation. So it may be helpful to keep in mind that stories of the soul can be told in various ways. Words are not the only way to communicate the power of truth inherent in our stories.

This caution surfaced for me when my religious community gathered in 1992 to discuss issues of grief and loss. In the small and large group conversations that took place during those days, it became quite clear that some people remained stoic and silent. Some of us presumed that they were in denial — that they had stuffed their pain and grief so deep into the suitcases of their psyches that no words could convey their sense of loss. Others suggested, however, that some of those who did not speak felt they were simply not articulate enough to adequately express what they wanted to say. So near the end of our time together, the facilitator suggested making two collages — one to depict where we felt we were right at that moment as a community and one that would capture our future. (This met with some resistance at first since many in my community do not have a bent toward such artistic expression.) Grudgingly, though, everyone participated. This gave those who had not said a word during the entire process an opportunity to cut and paste and plaster on the collages where they thought we were as a community and where they believed we would be in the future.

The exercise affirmed that each of us has a story to tell. Just because a person who gathers at the well remains silent doesn't mean he or she isn't engaged in the process. Remember the adage, "Still waters run deep." If we are blind to the truth of this old adage, we may shut off the flow of the Spirit and so deny ourselves the richness of the other's history, blessing and beauty.

At the rest stops of the soul, we must be willing to listen to each others' stories even when someone is not able to articulate the story or put her or his truth into words. We can learn much about such persons by paying attention to the silent language, the body language, of those who are silent when the stories are being told. By being attentive not only to the words spoken but the truth being told in a person's body language, we will begin to sense how in the well behind that person's eyes, there may be tears. When we trust one another enough, the bucket goes down and brings these tears to the surface. It is important to drink from these wells of experience — to savor each others' stories. And it is important to be creative in finding a variety of outlets for people to tell their stories.

The collage gave us a visual representation of how we saw ourselves and where we visioned we were going. For the most part, it filled us with great hope.

So when we gather around the wells at those rest stops of our lives, always remember to bring a large bucket. For when we stop by a well or a waterfall, sit for a spell and fill our very large hearts with the life-giving water of our stories, these large buckets, these very large hearts of ours, will once again be brimming with stories of hope, stories of God. Then, as we all gather at the well, drawing hope and spilling stories, we will come to know each other and God. And we will find refreshment for our thirsty souls.

INCIDENTS AND EXPECTATIONS OF INCARNATION

Chapter Six

Say to those whose hearts are frightened:
BE STRONG, FEAR NOT!
Here is your God. . .God comes to save you!
Then will the eyes of the blind be opened —
the ears of the deaf be cleared;
then will the lame leap like a stag —
then the tongue of the dumb will sing.

– Isaiah 35: 4-6

As important as it is to tell the stories of our ancestors, we also need to tell those stories from the experiences of today that remind us in small but significant ways that God is with us on this trail of transformation. We call these tales "incarnation stories" because they remind us that "God is with us." They surface for us the truth that no matter how discouraged we may become from sitting in dry wells, God is not discouraged. These incidents of incarnation also reflect the wonder of the Divine Presence in our very human lives as we walk in faith to the promised land of God's dreams for us.

The goal of incarnation stories is to bridge the distance between the sacred and the so-called secular areas of our lives; to see how the sacred stories of God illuminate and give a sense of direction to our worldly pursuits. Sadly, our tendency is to remove liturgy and the stories told and celebrated there from daily life. When we do this, we stifle the power that incarnation myths can have in shaping our response to the presence of the Divine Spirit among us.

A Place to Gather

Stories of God's incarnation are told at the various rest stops of the soul, when we gather in the company of friends. Whether we gather around a table in a cathedral or at the corner cafe, stories of incarnation reveal how the holy influences our very human struggles. These stories consecrate our connections with others by reminding us that we never walk alone.

This sense of connection found in incarnation stories surfaced for me last summer when I travelled to Denver to spend some time with a good friend. Rather than following Interstate 70 all the way, which would have been the most direct route, I took a different road. After all, I figured that's what vacations are for, to exit the fast lane and spend a few days travelling in the slow lane. The interstate is for people in a hurry to get where they were going. Although I was looking forward to spending time with my friend in the mountains, the blue highways provided a more scenic view of the Kansas skyscrapers — silos and grain elevators, storage bins and water towers — that told me another town was on the horizon. Or maybe I took the slow lane to pay homage to the late Charles Kuralt who had died a few days before I left for vacation. Kuralt spent his life on the road, listening to and telling the stories of ordinary people.

I stopped the first night in a small town in Western Kansas. Storm clouds were gathering in the west, and it seemed wise to rest. The little motel in this tiny town only took cash or checks, no credit cards, but it offered a comfortable room for a very reasonable rate.

The next morning I went across the highway for breakfast at the local restaurant. After ordering coffee, I looked at the clock on the wall: 6:00 AM. Since my watch and my body told me it was 7:00, I asked the waitress if that was the correct time. Then it dawned on me, I had crossed into mountain time. Though the mountains wouldn't come into view for another three or four hours, I had an extra hour. The first gift of this time away: the gift of time itself. An extra hour.

So I spent that hour eavesdropping on the conversations that were going on around me. Yes, even at that early hour, the cafe was crowded with farmers and ranchers. I imagine that these folks find their way to this gathering place almost every morning for breakfast and conversation. They talk about the weather and the price of wheat. They share percentages measured by their rain gauges: "Only got an eighth of an inch last night." These conversations are better than the morning newspaper. After they have exhausted the topics of crops and cattle, weather and wheat, they move on to other matters.

This particular morning they were fascinated by the pictures being sent back from Mars. When a new person came in the door, he was greeted like an old friend. With the arrival of every new member who joined this morning meeting, the talk returned to weather and the price of wheat. "Morning, did you get any rain up your way last night?" Evidently storms had plagued the area the past several days. They spoke in hushed tones of a man who lost his crop because of hail damage.

There were two large groups having separate meetings. But both knew each other well. In fact, one guy paid for everyone's breakfast at both tables. A simple "Thanks, Roy" sufficed. They all wore caps advertising farm implements or seed companies. I was somewhat surprised when I noticed one of them wearing Nike tennis shoes.

Western Kansas is flat land but there's nothing flat about these morning meetings. They are the gatherings that characterize community. The people here live on such large tracts of land, isolated from one another, that waking early and having coffee at this cafe keeps the connections and strengthens the bonds.

When I left the cafe to continue the journey to the mountains, I noticed a sign that pointed north: "Goodland." That name pretty well describes this part of the country: good land. It's land that stretches flat and wide, beyond eye's sight. It's land that provides for a good life and a livelihood. It's land where good friends gather at the cafe on a Monday morning to take care of the business of life.

The Good Life

This experience reminded me how we need places and people in our lives that help us take care of the business of life by helping us let go of the busyness of life — at least for an hour or even a few minutes. These places, these people become rest stops for the soul where stories of incarnation are told.

Jesus often tried to provide such rest stops for his disciples. Recall in Mark's Gospel: Jesus' friends have just returned from their first missionary activity. They are filled with stories of the road. They gather around Jesus to tell him "all that they had done and taught" (6: 30). I expect they also want to tell him about all they had seen and heard and learned. So Jesus advises them to "come away by yourselves to an out-of-the-way place and rest a while" (6: 31).

In these rest stops for the soul, we tell the stories of the road. In these rest stops for the soul, we listen to one another and learn a bit more about the business of life. In these rest stops for the soul, we let go of what needs to be done, if only for a little while, we slow the pace and embrace the truth that in our haste to make a living we sometimes forget to make a life. In our hurry to get to where we're going we sometimes miss the sights and sounds, the people and places we pass along the way.

When we are pulled apart by our work, in our relationships, in our activism for issues that are close to our hearts, we need every now and then to find a rest stop where we can pull ourselves together. We need to find an "out-of-the-way" place in our own backyard or by a lake or at a park to "rest awhile." When we are stretched in so many different directions, as elastic as our heart may be and as resilient as our spirit may be, we still need time by ourselves to get our life together or else the elasticity will be stretched to a breaking point. And when that band of love breaks, our souls stall.

Most of us only spend time at these rest stops once or twice a year during the period we have marked on our calendars in large letters: VACATION. When that time arrives and we hit the road to get away from it all, sometimes we maintain the pace we keep during the rest of the year. When we return we often seem more tired than when we left. But every now and then during this sacred space of leisure — whether we put our feet up as we gaze at majestic mountains in the early morning mist or soothe our thirsty feet in a cool stream; or put our feet under the table of a comfortable cafe in the company of friends — we may find ourselves whispering, "Ah, the good life."

The challenge, I suspect, comes in keeping that whisper alive in our hearts when the rubber meets the road again and we find ourselves rushing off to our next appointment. The challenge is to find these holy places of rest in the midst of the hectic pace of everyday life. The challenge is to take a few mini-vacations each day to refresh the spirit and restore the soul. As Rabbi Harold Kushner reminds us, the primary meaning of Sabbath, which reflects this sense of the sacred space of leisure, is to "retrieve the soul." Vacation time is Sabbath time. Vacation time is soul time.

Breaking the Fast Pace

We try to build these soul times into our schedule each day, don't we? Or at least many of us used to. Three times a day, morning, noon, and evening, we are invited to take some soul time. We eat breakfast, a word which means breaking the fast we've experienced during sleep. It also could imply "breaking the fast pace" the day will tempt us to keep. We have a "lunch hour," which — even though it has usually been reduced to a "lunch half-hour" or less due to the premium we place on productivity — encourages us to pause in the middle of the day to rest awhile. Of course, in this age of "power lunches" the busyness of life has replaced the business of enjoying life. We also have the "dinner hour," a time designed to tell the stories of the day in the company of those we love the most. However, this soul time is often squeezed out by the work of the day that never seems to end or by evening activities that crowd our schedules. Yet as Mahatma Gandhi said, "There is more to life than increasing its speed," to which Henry David Thoreau would add, "As if you could kill time without injuring eternity."

When these rest stops in the course of our day are bypassed or become a blur, a fading image in our rearview mirror, in the high-speed chase that characterizes so many of our lives, there is little chance for the stories of incarnation to be told. When we fail to take the time to tell the stories at these rest stops which are built into each day's map, we are diminished. We miss the opportunity to hear how the presence of God was made manifest at school or at work or at the grocery store. By neglecting these stories with their timely reminders of God's incarnation in our daily lives, we gradually lose our sense of the sacred. We become dulled by the routine of endless work; our soul begins to lose its edge. And when we lose our edge of awareness of how God is always present among us, we tend to relegate God to times of formal worship and so miss the divine thread that weaves through our lives.

Perhaps there's no better symbol of our fast-paced age than the fast-food restaurants that crowd the corridors of every city and town. After all, have you ever heard of a slow-food restaurant? With all the activities that clutter our calendars, it's no wonder most of us need at least one extended vacation each year.

This hectic pace of life is not new. Indeed, it is evident in the very passage in Mark's Gospel when, after Jesus invites the disciples to come away to a deserted place to rest awhile, the people hurry after them. Some even arrive ahead of them. So many people, so many needs, so many appointments to keep, the Gospel says, that Jesus and the disciples "had no leisure even to eat" (6: 31).

Most of us can relate to this experience.

So, what can we do? Maybe that's not the question. Perhaps the question that will strengthen the sense of balance between rest and work for which our souls and bodies, minds and spirits yearn is not about doing anything but about being someone who tends to and cares for one's own soul first. For only when our own souls are healed can we meet others in their souls' needs.

Jesus tried to tend to the souls of his disciples. He tried to create a break in the fast pace of their missionary lives. But he couldn't get away from the crowds completely. They kept coming for more of the soul food they found in him that nourished their spirits. Still, he kept a primary place in his daybook for the need to stop and rest awhile.

BALANCING ACT: BEING BROUGHT NEAR

For most of us, however, this balancing act is difficult. In the busyness of life, we so often find ourselves on lonely stretches of road where there are no services for miles and miles.

A couple of hours after I left that cafe where the farmers and ranchers were telling their stories, I turned on a road marked with the sign: NO SERVICES 70 MILES. No rest stops. No service stations. Traveling this stretch of road, I saw a sign that mentioned the next Colorado town. It was called Rush. I wondered if there were any services in Rush and thought to myself, "I'd better hurry." About halfway through this stretch of road without services, I regretted I'd drunk so much coffee at breakfast. Checking my gas gauge, it was clear to me that at the next service station

I saw I would have to fill the car's tank and empty mine.

On the trail of transformation, we are often like people hurrying along the highways and byways of life without any services for miles. We are like the people in Mark's Gospel who hurried to that "lonely place" where Jesus was taking his disciples to rest awhile. When Jesus saw the crowd, "he had compassion on them, because they were like sheep without a shepherd (6: 34)." Jesus' compassion took the form of storytelling as he "began to teach them many things." Maybe he taught them the need to take some time to rest awhile. Maybe he taught them how to balance their lives between leisure and labor. Certainly he taught them what it takes to live "a good life" — a life that integrates and seeks to balance the pressing demands that crowd our lives.

For these people who seemed so scattered, Jesus himself became a rest stop for the soul. They listened to his stories and found some rest, found some balance, found some strength for the road that stretched ahead of them.

Jesus' attended to the peoples' needs by tending to their souls. He refreshed their spirits by taking the time to tell the stories of the good life. He came out of his solitude to create a sacred space where community could be found, where the remnant could find some rest, where the fearful and faltering might find some strength for the journey. Like those farmers and ranchers gathering at the local cafe on a Monday morning, Jesus created a meeting place where souls are tended, spirits find rest and remnants find a home.

As we walk this trail of transformation, it is important to check the map on the blue highways of our lives and note those places and people where we find a little rest for our weary souls. After all, we never know when we might come upon a stretch of the road with the sign: NO SERVICES.

The Primary Incarnation Story: God is With Us

As God looked upon the vast expanse of the earth, perhaps it was this sign, NO SERVICES, that prompted God to respond with another sign. As God looked with compassion upon the scattered remnant, upon human beings bent low by oppression and bent out of shape by the hectic pace of life, upon a style of living where all the stations in life were "self-service," or self-serving rather than serving the rest, God decided to replace the old signs with a new one. It was a sign remarkable in its simplicity, eternal in its consequences.

This sign, found in the primary incarnation story of the Christian canon, is foretold by Isaiah (7: 14) when the prophet writes about a young woman having a baby. The prophet says this child shall be called Immanuel, a name which means "God is with us." The story says that no matter how desperate we become, no matter how forsaken we feel, no matter how weary we are, God still hopes in us; God still dreams in us. It is an image that is echoed with the birth of each child as the miracle of life eclipses the mystery of death.

This incarnation myth from our faith story becomes relevant when we understand how it is being lived out today. Here is a story that tells us how it happens. Here is an example of an incarnation myth that gives us courage to survive those seasons of drought. It's a story that helps us endure those seemingly eternal moments when the muse is missing, when our lives seem out of rhyme or when the rhythm of our heart skips more than a beat. It is an image that is recycled every liturgical year; an image that reminds us that God is not discouraged.

The Nesbit family didn't seem particularly blessed, but they certainly weren't cursed either. They were a very ordinary family with three children, a father who drank a little too much and a mother whose deep faith fashioned the foundation of their family life. For many years they experienced a rather carefree existence. There were some setbacks and more than a few sorrows, like the death of Mr. Nesbit's mother. But she had lived a long life and her death was marked by serenity and acceptance. That was one of the rare times the Nesbits had to look closely at the face of death, and they came through the experience with more memories of her life than fears about death.

But Mr. Nesbit began to drink more than a little too much, and as the children grew older they slowly began to realize he had signs of alcoholism. However, he never missed a day at work and rarely drank during the week. The family simply accepted the fact that every weekend Mr. Nesbit would nurse a couple of cases of beer and talk to imaginary friends in the garage. When one of the children would suggest that their dad had a drinking problem, Mrs. Nesbit would shrug off the notion of confronting her husband about his lost weekends.

The three Nesbit children were popular and outgoing. They excelled in their school work, especially John, the oldest, who was his father's favorite. John was an outstanding athlete, and that coupled with his academic achievements won him a scholarship to college. After college, he settled into a job which earned him a substantial salary.

Karen, the oldest daughter, married a man her parents disliked at first. He was a conscientious objector during the Vietnam War, and since Mr. Nesbit was a veteran of the Korean War, he thought conscientious objection was just a fancy name for "coward." After Karen and Mike were married, however, and the family grew to know Mike's deep convictions, they accepted him. Mr. Nesbit and Mike agreed to disagree about the war, and the topic was rarely discussed.

1979 was a banner year for the Nesbits. They moved to a larger house in a more fashionable neighborhood, and Mr. and Mrs. Nesbit celebrated their twenty-fifth wedding anniversary. That was the year Karen and Mike were married and Kenny, the youngest son, graduated from high school. Everything seemed to be going well. There was nothing extraordinary, just an ordinary family enjoying life's moments of passage and trying to deal with the minor conflicts with a large dose of patience and perseverance.

However, the next year their ordinary life began to unravel. John, the oldest son, took an overdose of drugs and almost died. What followed was a long period of withdrawal from the drugs he had been taking since high school. Unknown to his family, John was an addict. Even after numerous attempts at treatment, John couldn't kick the habit. He lost his job and moved to another city. The family rarely heard from him except when he needed money.

The discovery of John's addiction was only the beginning. Because his favorite son had deceived him, Mr. Nesbit began to drink even more. One day he was fired from his job and that night drove his car off the road. He was in the hospital for two months, and the injuries sustained in the accident along with his continued drinking kept him at home most of the time.

This created even more tensions within the house. He would get into violent arguments with his youngest son, Kenny. One day, he threw Kenny out of the house. Kenny quit college and joined the army. He was so angry with his father that he vowed to his mother the day he left that he would never set foot in the house again.

Then, in early 1981, Mr. and Mrs. Nesbit received a call late at night telling them that John, their oldest son, was dead. Police found him in an alley and speculated that a drug deal had gone awry.

Within a short span of time, the ordinary Nesbit family was shaken by extraordinary events and circumstances. John's death colored their lives with anger, doubt and fear. A family that had once been so close and seemingly immune to tragedy was now overwhelmed by forces beyond their control. The boundaries of their safe and secure existence had been shattered. The family scattered.

FINDING MEANING IN THE INCARNATION

We stop the story there because it is at this point where the prophet Isaiah's words find their deepest meaning. "Behold a young woman shall conceive and bear a son and shall call his name Immanuel" (7: 14). It took a bold and daring voice to utter these words, for they were born in the midst of chaos and confusion. The bright promise given to Abraham and Sarah and passed on to Isaac and Jacob and Joseph, the promise of land given to the prophet Moses, a land where the people could enjoy peace and security — these promises had been broken not by God but by a string of unjust and ruthless kings who were willing to sell their people into slavery in return for personal privilege and honor. Isaiah in this passage is confronting one of those kings, Ahaz, who has already decided to surrender to the enemy armies waiting to take over Jerusalem. Isaiah condemns the king's cowardice and reminds him that even though all avenues for peace have been exhausted, one had yet to be tried: trust in God.

True to the nature of a prophet, Isaiah reminds the king that the nation was built on the covenantal relationship between God and the people. Though their history has been marked by numerous examples of the nation's infidelity and sin, God has remained faithful. Isaiah plants the seed of hope once again in the hearts of the people: Their nation will survive if they place their faith in God. And this will be a sign: A young woman will give birth to a child and that child will give them a new future.

Isaiah did not panic in the face of chaos but drew upon the vision that God alone can save. To sustain the people in their most desperate moment of loss, Isaiah told the creation story again. He taught the people and their king a basic lesson in hope: Wait for the signs of new life to appear even amid the desolation of the present moment.

This image of God, Immanuel, means that God is with us even in the aftermath of shattered dreams, even in the turbulent times of tragedy, even in the bruises and blows of a battered life. It takes exceptional vision to whisper the name Immanuel when we are confronted with loneliness and loss brokenness and betrayal, sickness and insanity, despair and death. Despite the desolation and despair, we can draw upon the riches of our tradition which has given us Abraham and Sarah's faith and Isaiah's vision of hope.

The incarnation story says that God comes to the world as an infant wrapped in a blanket and born in a manger. God comes to the earth as a fragile child who is full of life; weak, yet full of wonder; dependent, yet full of dreams. The story suggests that even though we are fragile, we can give life to another. Though we are weak, we can celebrate the wonders of God's love. Though we are dependent, we can give birth to new dreams.

On November 18, 1983, this story took a new and deeper meaning for the Nesbit family. Karen gave birth to a baby girl. They gave her the name Jennifer, but her name is the same as that of every other newborn child: Immanuel. For Jennifer's life told the Nesbit family that even in the darkness of John's death, even in the chaos caused by alcoholism, even in the storms of anger and resentment, God was with them. God was not discouraged. God was there even in the scars and suffering they had endured.

RAISING EXPECTATIONS

Incarnation stories inspire us to raise our expectations of ourselves, our families, our faith communities, our world. When we think about our sometimes elusive attitudes about our expectations, a question comes to mind. When do we give up our best dreams, our highest hopes, our greatest expectations for ourselves, our families, friends, communities and our world? Is there a moment when we come to realize that what we once dreamed for ourselves would not come true? Is there a time we can pinpoint when we knew we'd have to lower our expectations?

I think I was a freshman in college when I concluded that the expectation of my youth that I would be the starting shortstop for the

St. Louis Cardinals would not be realized. So I didn't even try out for the Rockhurst College baseball team. Since I was in the seminary and we had Mass in the afternoon at the same time the team practiced, I didn't even bother my director with the possibility of skipping Mass to play ball.

At what point in our lives do we stop expecting to win an Academy Award or a Pulitzer Prize or placing a Nobel Prize for literature, medicine or peace on our mantle?

When do we lower our expectations about the world that one day we will learn to live in peace and learn war no more? When do we lower our expectations that the violence, oppression and injustice in our society will be eliminated? When do we lose our expectations altogether about some of the dreams we've had for our church, for equal status and gender justice in our faith community?

When do we lower our expectations of ourselves about making a difference in this world, our community, our church? When do we lower our expectations about each other — about our ability to change, to grow, to deepen our love?

When do we lower our expectations about God?

Incarnation stories give us an answer to those questions about lowering expectations. The answer is: Never!

Oh, we may have moments of doubt as we try to muster courage for the journey that is ahead of us. But this doubt shouldn't disturb us. After all, one of the great players in our Incarnation stories, John the Baptist, even had some uncertainty about the coming of the Messiah. Remember the story of John sitting in his cell and sending his disciples to ask Jesus, "Are you the one who is to come, or should we expect another?" (Matthew 11: 3). Does this surprise us that the one so identified with preparing the way for the coming of the Messiah might have doubts about the one he spent his life preaching about? Was he expecting a different kind of Messiah — not a gentle, healing, poetic preacher but one who, like himself, would spew fire and brimstone from the furnace of his heart? Was the one whose life formed a bridge between the old and new, the one whose prophecies spanned the chasm of time between Isaiah and Jesus, having second thoughts or lowering his expectations about the coming of the Messiah?

In raising the expectations of John and his disciples, Jesus doesn't come right out and say, "Yes, I'm the Messiah." Instead, he challenges them to open their ears and eyes to hear and see the signs that are happening in their midst: "the blind receive their sight, the lame walk, the lepers are cleansed, the deaf hear, the dead are raised, and the poor have good news brought to them" (Matthew 11: 4-5).

Isaiah's Expectations

These are the same signs the prophet Isaiah pointed to in Chapter 35 (4-6) when he wrote:

> Say to those whose hearts are frightened:
> BE STRONG, FEAR NOT!
> Here is your God. . .God comes to save you!
> Then will the eyes of the blind be opened —
> the ears of the deaf be cleared;
> then will the lame leap like a stag —
> then the tongue of the dumb will sing . . . .

The prophet visualized his age in the imagery of a desert. As we know from reading the Gospels, Jesus patterned his life, and his response to the evil in his world, after the model of Isaiah's suffering servant. Isaiah challenged the existing structures of his day at the same time as he offered comfort to the people oppressed by those structures. He named the sin while giving comfort to those broken by sin. Chapter 35 of Isaiah offers ten verses of sheer hope. Verses which proclaim a vision for the people to embrace. Verses which serve as a map for our mystical journey through life.

It is important to remember that the people to whom Isaiah was speaking were suffering exile and captivity. They had been reduced to a remnant. Their lives resembled a barren and parched wasteland. What were they expecting? They were expecting death. They were not only expecting death, they were praying for it. They were experiencing the depths of depression that few of us can even imagine. They were a people filled with an overwhelming sense of hopelessness because they had been torn away from their homeland and made slaves. They had been brutalized and beaten, robbed and raped, used and abused beyond description. They had been treated as garbage, dehumanized and defeated. So oppressed, so broken, what else could they expect but death?

What else could they desire but death? They welcomed death because at least death would end their suffering.

To these people, Isaiah says: "Be strong, do not fear! Here is your God!" (Isaiah 35: 4).

After all, he says, what did you expect?

The image is this: In the desert of what had become their lives, flowers will grow. In this soil rich in suffering, new blossoms will take root and bloom. For these people who are parched, whose lives resemble a barren, forsaken wasteland, the prophet paints a picture of hope.

Isaiah tells these people whose eyes have been blinded by fear that they will see the glorious vision of a savior. He tells these people whose ears have heard nothing but the deafening clang of chains that they will listen to the joyful sounds of celebration. To these people whose legs have buckled under the weight of injustice, he proposes that they will dance freely in the court of their king. To these people whose backs have been twisted by torture, whose tongues have been silenced by utter despair, he says that they will sing without ceasing.

After all, what did you expect?

The prophet smashes the downward spiral of our expectations and not only raises them but brings them to a new level beyond our wildest dreams.

EXPECTATIONS OF LIFE

The basic questions incarnation stories confront us with are these: What do we expect of God? and What do we expect of ourselves? Our ongoing conversion can be framed within our responses to those two questions.

One of the saddest homilies I've ever heard was given by one of the members of my religious community on the occasion of his fortieth anniversary as a priest. He began his homily by telling us that the one thing he has learned in forty years as a priest is, "Lower your expectations." We laughed because this man was known for his humor, and we thought he was using that line as a lure to pull us in to some happy recollections of his life as a priest. Instead, he used that line as a refrain after recounting his numerous disappointments as a member of the congregation. He told us stories of run-ins with provincials and being sent to places on the far fringe of the province. When he concluded his homily by advising us to "lower our expectations," the stillness in the church reflected a deep sadness in all who heard this wounded priest tell his story.

Unlike the picture painted by that priest, Isaiah's vision encourages us to live beyond our expectations about life. A true story may help us put in proper perspective our own expectations of this life to which we have been called:

Many years ago in a mental institution outside Boston, there was a young girl known as "Little Annie." She was locked in a dungeon because the doctors had determined that Little Annie was hopelessly insane. Since they saw little possibility for progress in her, she was confined to a small cell in the dungeon that received very little light.

In many ways Little Annie was like an animal. At times, she would violently attack a person who came into her cage. At other times, she would huddle and hide in a corner, completely ignoring the visitor.

There happened to be on staff at the time an elderly nurse who was nearing retirement. Because in her many years at the hospital this nurse had seen even the most hopeless cases make some progress, she decided to invest some of her time with Little Annie. She would go down to the dungeon and eat her lunch outside Little Annie's cage. She would talk to the little girl even though Little Annie gave no hint that she was aware the nurse was there. The nurse believed just by her presence she could communicate some warmth, love and maybe some hope to the little girl.

One evening before she went home, the nurse left a plate of brownies outside Little Annie's cell. When the nurse returned the next day, the brownies were gone. From that time one, once a week, on Thursday evening, the nurse would leave brownies for Little Annie. It wasn't long before the doctors noticed a change taking place in Little Annie's behavior. She became more responsive. In fact, she made so much progress that the doctors decided to move Little Annie upstairs. She made even more progress, remarkable progress, and after a long period of time, this girl, once deemed a "hopeless case," was told she could go home.

But Little Annie stayed. She never forgot the compassion shown to her by that elderly nurse who brought her the plate of brownies every Thursday evening. Little Annie decided that she would help someone else like the nurse had helped her. She decided to adopt another "hopeless case." And that is what she did. She cared for, taught and nurtured a young girl named Helen Keller.

You see, "Little Annie" was Anne Sullivan.

Seasons of the Heart

Think of Little Annie, alone, forsaken, destined to die in that dungeon; think of the countless people today paralysed by fear because of the ever-tightening vise of violence; think of those wounded by a love that has been lost or broken by the betrayal of a beloved; think of those imprisoned on death row, their appeals exhausted; think of those who are homeless, weighed down by the indifference of others; think of those whose hearts were once so generous but after having been used once too often have now turned as hard as concrete, who are unable to trust or even to care; think of those who are dying alone, without even one person to mourn their passing; then hear what the story of the incarnation asks: "What do we expect of God? What to we expect of ourselves?"

The first question is answered in Jesus' response to John the Baptist's disciples. Jesus answers their question with another question: "What do you see?" (Matthew 11: 4). What do we see, we who live at the advent of the twenty-first century? Do we see we are more caring and less callous? Do we see we are more forgiving and less begrudging? Do we see we are more compassionate and less apathetic?

Then consider what others see when they see us. Do they see that the Messiah has already come in the attitudes and actions that shape our lives?

Isn't this all we expect of God — to stay with us, to call forth from us greater love, deeper commitment, larger hope? Isn't this what we expect of ourselves — to be for one another what that nurse was for Little Annie; what Annie became for Helen Keller? Don't we expect, as Isaiah's prophecy suggested, that we will draw each other out of our dungeons of diminished expectations about life, that we will give each other a little more hope to keep us going, keep us growing?

Yes, we expect this but even more! For believing that God is in our midst, we expect the eyes of the blind shall be opened and the ears of the deaf unstopped; we expect the lame will dance and the tongues of the speechless will sing for joy. Yes, we expect more surprises from this God of ours because we believe God's Spirit continues to stir our souls, creating within our hearts profound expectations of the kind we never even dreamed.

At those rest stops of the soul where incarnation stories are told, we are invited to learn the lessons of the seasons of the heart even as we raise our expectations of ourselves, of each other and of God. Though some of our dreams will be buried under a blanket of snow and not survive the winter's cold; though some of our hopes will fall like leaves from the trees and for awhile seem dead and gone; though some of our expectations will wither from lack of moisture or attention, stories of incarnation invite us to sense a groaning and a growing beneath our feet and inside our souls. With the gift of patience guarding our lives, we stand with active anticipation for the coming of our God in new and exciting ways as we seek to live the vision of Isaiah and the message of Jesus.

Incarnation stories advise us never to lower our expectations of God, of ourselves, of one another, of our faith communities or of our world. By placing our trust in God rather than in our own expectations, we shall see how our hope grows beyond our wildest dreams.

Hope for the Future

When we share incidents of incarnation at these rest stops of the soul, we model for each other, for our descendants in family and community life, hope for the future. Isn't it true that every generation wants to provide a better, safer, more loving world for the next generation? We want to provide a world that includes possibilities for peace and potential for joy. We have such capacity within us, but it takes time and it takes risk. The risk is to believe in our own goodness and the goodness of others. The risk is to trust our own truth, our own story, and the risk is to tell our story, our truth, to others. The risk is to not give in to the temptation to give up. The risk is to never be satisfied with the way we love but to love even more.

In the language of the soul, love is written not in words but in glances. Love is expressed by one's body, one's movement — a lighter step, a livelier appearance. We cannot hide love's truth: It is written in bold letters on our faces, in our eyes and in the freedom of our embrace with those with whom we share our story.

At the rest stops of the soul where incarnation stories are told, we live a delicate balance of knowing when to speak out and when to be silent. We walk a fine line of knowing what words to say, what stories to tell, and what tales to keep to ourselves. In this tension, there is life. Abundant life. It is this belief in life that incarnation stories convey. This belief becomes the promise and the passion that shapes us and molds us into being poets of our own truth. As we pursue our pilgrimage of transformation along the sometimes steep slopes of suffering and sorrow, it is this belief in life that will keep us on our feet. Though we may fall from grace or fall out of favor from time to time, the incidents of incarnation we carry in our travelling bag remind us that from God's perspective we will always fall on the side of life.

THE QUEST FOR VISION

Chapter Seven

The fear of the unknown and the lure of the comfortable will conspire to keep you from taking the chances the traveler needs to take. But if you take them, you will never regret your choice. To be sure, there will be moments of doubt when you stand alone on an empty road in an icy rain, or when you are ill with fever in a rented bed. But as the pains of the moment will come, so too will they fall away. In the end, you will be so much richer, so much stronger, so much clearer, so much happier, and so much better a person that all the risk and hardship will seem like nothing compared to the knowledge and wisdom you have gained.

– Kent Nerburn, *Letters to My Son*, New World Library, 1994

There is no other true wisdom except that which comes from the Holy Spirit and that wisdom is given only to the humble.

– St. Francis de Sales

We carry the incarnation vision of abundant, eternal life close to our hearts as we walk the trail of transformation. The incarnation story of the Christian tradition says that this is the reason God became human, the reason God's Word became flesh in the person of Jesus: so that all who believe may have eternal life. At the rest stops of the soul, we trace this movement of life in the direction of God's goodness and proclaim it boldly, without compromise, to our companions along the way.

Incidents of incarnation reflect the presence of God among us and so awaken us to our own goodness and the goodness that is present in others. Our own incarnation stories, those moments when God's Word became flesh in the language of our lives, strengthen these sacred connections that bind us together as good and holy people of life. In this chapter, we will explore three metaphors — the mall, the health food store and the mountain — that reflect God's vision of abundant life and the challenges inherent in living fully within this vision. These three metaphors become rest stops on the trail of transformation where incidents of incarnation stretch our souls and strengthen our resolve to be involved in this vision quest.

The Mall: The Upside of Downsizing

Recently, I've noticed an interesting place where incarnation stories are being told: the shopping mall. One morning I arrived early at the mall because I was running late. You see, it was my mother's birthday and I hadn't gotten her a gift yet. I was driving across the state to begin a retreat that evening in my home town, and I wanted to stop and see my mom that afternoon on my way. So I arrived at the mall at 8:30 A.M. to find a present. But since I don't hang around malls very much, I didn't know that most stores in most malls don't open until 9:30. So, in the violent metaphor of today, I had an hour to *kill*.

I decided, however, to use a different metaphor and *spend* an hour watching people. And there were lots of people in the mall. There were mainly older people — many of them walking, others talking around tables at one of the few establishments open, a small cafe. Others were sitting on benches carrying on conversations, catching their friends up on the news about children or grandchildren. One seemed very serious, as if he were telling the other some very disturbing news he had received from his doctor. For the most part, however, the talking was lighthearted and the walking lightfooted. It appeared to be a good way to begin a day: The walking provided good exercise for the body; the talking afforded good exercise for the soul.

I don't want to suggest that malls have replaced churches as places where people go to nourish their souls. Yet I do think the metaphor of the mall, like that cafe in the small town in western Kansas where ranchers and farmers gathered early in the morning, reminds us of the need for those sacred spaces in our lives where we feel at home enough to tell our stories. We need sacred soul spaces where we can tell and hear those tales of wonder and of woe that tap our deepest fears and highest hopes, stories that not only transfigure us but transform us.

In an era when many major corporations are "downsizing" to produce larger profits and higher numbers on the stock exchange — at the expense, of course, of employees who are laid off — many faith communities are doing just the opposite. We are closing or combining or clustering small parishes in inner cities and rural areas while at the same time creating new "super" communities in the suburbs. In a sense, we are responding to the "mall" mentality of our culture that sees small, family-owned businesses in our downtown areas suffer at the expense of larger, more convenient shopping experiences in the malls.

Yet in the journey of conversion there is a need for downsizing — the heart-full rather than the heart-less variety. The upside of downsizing comes in understanding what it means to be catalysts for conversion and agents of transformation in the communities of faith where we are privileged to serve. This kind of downsizing means going down to the depth of our lives, our experiences, our expectations. On the path of transformation, we do not *grow up* but rather seek to *grow down*, to get in touch again with those primary, foundational truths of our lives. This growing down is a tedious but transforming process that results in discovery: the discovery of God's truth.

We can carry this metaphor of the mall a bit further by reflecting on what we find in many of the stores that make up a mall: new clothes. In the process we can begin to sense the invitation and the challenge of downsizing. For example, numerous advertising adages speak to our need to "dress for success," implying that "we are what we wear." Clothes convey much information about the person who wears them. So how might we "dress for success" on the trip of our lifetime: the journey of transforma-tion? Where might we shop to find the right clothes to reflect our desire for divine downsizing?

Well, imagine a unique boutique at the mall called Isaiah's. It's a place where we shop until we drop to a smaller size. Old Isaiah becomes our fashion consultant for the journey of transformation. Isaiah is the out-fitter for adventuresome souls who seek to explore the depths of life.

In Chapter 11, verse 5, Isaiah suggests that instead of one of those indigo scarves that can accent any outfit, a soul explorer will purchase justice to be a "band around his (her) waist." Isaiah promises that this band of justice will hold everything together in style.

Need a new belt to hold up those pants? Try faithfulness. According to the prophet, you will never be caught with your pants down.

Acknowledging how children of God tend to grow so quickly, our fashion consultant also announces a new line of children's clothes (Isaiah 11: 6-7). The prophet calls it the Petting Zoo Collection, and it captures the menagerie and mystery of downsizing: a turtleneck with a wolf and lamb walking together, a shirt that instead of having an alligator insignia has a leopard and a kid resting together, a cap with a calf and a young lion browsing together, a jacket with a cow and a bear exchanging glances.

This is Isaiah's vision of the taming of the wild kingdom to come. In this kingdom, all are children. In fact, a child is the holy ringmaster of this circus called community. There's a child playing in the cobra's den and still another laying a hand on the adder's lair.

This new fashion line presented by Isaiah is possible when "the earth is filled with the knowledge of God" (11: 9).

Now, I can hear you protest that these clothes just won't fit. They are too small. You're probably right; they are too small. But that means it's time we grow *down*. It's time we lose some weight: the weight of indifference that has gathered around our waist, or the heaviness we feel around our heart for holding grudges too long. It's time to shed the extra pounds of self-pity that produce a sluggish soul or those pounds of pride that fill the barrel of our chest, making it harder to breathe. It's time to rid ourselves of that albatross of anger that hangs around our neck or that attitude of fear that keeps us from sticking our neck out for truth and justice.

Spiritual Health Food Store: Hope and Humility

To facilitate this necessary weight loss, we notice that right next to Isaiah's boutique in the mall there is a health food store. There we find a diet plan prescribed by our divine physician that insures sufficient weight loss to fit into these new clothes for the adventurous road of transformation. The diet plan is simple: Drink as much hope and eat as much humble pie as possible. The intake of hope will circulate through our bodies to break up those clots of compromise and caution that accumulate in our arteries and cause us to be lethargic and listless. The humble pie we eat for dessert has very few calories and makes us feel small again.

Of course, humble pie is hard to swallow. A few years ago I read an article by Archbishop John Quinn of San Francisco entitled "It is the best of times to be a priest." At the time, I thought it was odd because almost daily we were being reminded of the scandals involving certain priests which tended to tarnish the image of every priest. Surveys of every sort were telling us that morale among priests was never lower. Many pastors were caught in the crossfire of criticism from the right and from the left. The lack of affirmation and the ambiguity of the present age made it difficult for many priests to think of this as the best of times. Indeed, Archbishop Quinn acknowledged this no-win situation many priests found themselves in by asking the question that crowded and clouded many a priest's mind and heart: "Why should anyone consider being a priest and why should any priest continue his priestly service in such a hostile and unsatisfying environment?"

One answer the archbishop gave in his article is summed up by the words of St. Francis de Sales: "There is no other true wisdom except that which comes from the Holy Spirit and that wisdom is given only to the humble."

As priestly people on the trail of transformation, this age provides a learning center for humility. To be a person of faith today is a humbling experience. Only, however, by embracing this virtue of humility can one learn wisdom. That is why Archbishop Quinn could write that this is the best of times to be a priest. That is why it is the best of times to be in a community of faith committed to conversion. We can thank God for the crucibles and crises, the potholes and detours we experience on the road because they remind us of what Pope Pius XI once said: "We live in these times when it is no longer permitted to anyone to be mediocre."

When we are serious about downsizing and fitting into the clothes of a new creation, we begin to see this upside of downsizing: that we must not permit each other to be mediocre. We must demand excellence because we do not have a mediocre Messiah but one who is willing to stand in our corner, to stand by our side, as we wrestle to bring redemption to our world. This Messiah of ours desires nothing more than to inspire us and lead us through our pain to the promised land of our dreams.

By drinking in hope and eating the humble pie that is often served us, we grow down while the child proclaimed in our primary incarnation story, Jesus Christ, grows up in our attitudes and actions. If we are ever going to fit into the new clothes of wisdom and understanding, counsel and strength, the clothes we hope to wear on the road of transformation, then we must learn to grow down. We must develop a taste for humble pie.

The main ingredient in both this hope and this humble pie is found in a natural herb we buy at the health food store, also owned and operated by Isaiah: "a shoot that sprouts from the stump of Jesse" (Isaiah 11: 1). In this bud that blossoms are the ingredients to make us young, small and childlike again. And the remarkable thing is that it doesn't matter what age we are. We can always take this medicine, follow this diet and see how God is getting us back in shape for the journey that lies ahead.

Take this story, for instance, which is drawn from an experience I had when I was in parish work, an incarnation story about visiting two women in a nursing home. Maggie's fingers were twisted and bent. Her hands were gnarled by time and arthritis. Maggie's mind, however, was sharp and her eyes burned with longing and love. When I walked into her room at the nursing home, the flowers and plants on her dresser reflected the life that flourished within Maggie's frail frame. Once, she pointed to one plant in particular and with more than a hint of pride told me how she had found it many years ago.

It was a tiny sprout on an eroding hillside being choked by rocks and baked by the sun. It was a magical seedling because by the laws of nature it should not have been growing in such a parched place. So Maggie carefully rescued it and repotted it. It gave her a symbol of life that she could take with her to the grave. "I've already told my daughter that I want that plant next to my tombstone," Maggie told me that day.

"On that day, a shoot shall sprout from the stump of Jesse." This prophecy of Isaiah captures what it means to hope even when surrounded by despair. We can identify with such a feeling, if we have experienced the pain of broken dreams, if we have known the hurt of a shattered relationship, if we have grieved the loss of someone we love.

There are many times in our lives, times of anguish and uncertainty, when the decision to hope or not to hope becomes clear. Maggie decided that, even though her life was almost over, there was no looking back at the failures of the past. Instead, she treasured the precious moments of her life and so fashioned a future for herself and those who knew her.

What happens, however, when hope dies? I didn't have to look very far for an answer. Even the vibrant energy of Maggie would wane in the company of her roommate at the nursing home. Martha's head would droop as she'd feign sleep. She wanted to ward off any unwelcome guests, and, in Martha's address book, that is everyone.

"Martha," I would say softly. "How are you today?"

There would be no response, but I knew her ploy well because I had visited her many times before. One day, I had more courage than usual, and I walked over to her wheelchair and sat on the bed. I touched her arm gently. "Martha." She looked up and her eyes were burning, but not with love.

"Get away from me!" she screamed.

But I held on.

"Can't you see I'm sleeping. Leave me alone!"

There were no flowers or plants on Martha's side of the room. A battered alarm clock on the top of her nightstand was her only contact with time. It told her story: It had stopped four hours ago.

Martha had to rewind it whenever she wanted the correct time. It was much like she had to rewind her life, which had stopped more than four years before when her only son moved to another city and left her in the nursing home. Her body was wasting away and bent over by the weight of loneliness; her hands were cold as they pushed my hands away. "Can't you hear? Go talk to her," she said sharply, referring to Maggie. "I don't want to talk to you."

My best instincts told me to go back to Maggie, but I said, "Martha, is there anything I can do for you?"

"No." Her anger began to melt her frosty heart. "Unless you want to pray to that God of yours to let me die. He doesn't seem to listen to me. All I want to do is die!"

It was certainly easier for me to recognize the face of God in Maggie than in Martha. Yet, our continuing conversion as children of God invites us to see God's presence in the lives and faces of both these women.

Only when we know and believe in this presence can we understand these women's stories. Only then can we share the joy that surrounds Maggie's blossoming life and give Martha a glimpse of hope, patiently helping her to break down the walls that keep her separate, distant and apart.

We do this by purchasing large quantities of those two priceless virtues we find at the spiritual health store: hope and humility. But please read the instructions on the label: The only way we can swallow humble pie is by washing it down with hope.

MOUNTAIN CLIMBING

The third metaphor that reveals incidents of incarnation is the familiar scriptural image of the mountain. In the biblical tradition, mountains are one of God's favorite meeting places. Evidence of divine revelation is seen in mountain stories concerning no less than Moses, Elijah, and Jesus. Indeed, these three central figures meet one day on a mountain in the story of the transfiguration (Matthew 17: 1-9).

The story tells of the day Jesus invited three of his closest friends to go mountain climbing. When they reached the summit, he was transfigured before their eyes. In the life of the three disciples who witnessed this remarkable vision, this was a peak experience. But as they soon discovered, it was all downhill from there. Still, this was a pinnacle moment to savor. It was one of those experiences in the course of one's life that lingers forever. The disciples could draw upon this view of life from the top of the mountain when they walked through the valley of death.

Last summer, a friend and I went to the mountains for a couple of days. The place where we stayed was on the crest of a ridge from which one could look and literally see mountains on every side. We were above the tree line, and the first thing we noticed when we arrived after more than doubling the altitude on the trip from Denver was how light-headed we felt.

On this mountain, with its snow-capped peaks fully in view, the question the psalmist once raised came to mind: "Where can I run from your love? If I climb to the mountains, you are there" (Psalm 139: 8). To me, nothing is more reflective of God's majesty than a mountain in dawn's early light. Such a view sends the soul to rare heights of wonder.

Our souls need a mountain view every now and then. Our souls need to seek new altitudes that will give us a wider view, a higher perspective. Such an altitude yields a new view — and maybe even a new attitude.

The higher we are, the farther the soul can see. Oh, this is not without danger — experienced mountain climbers attest to this. From the privileged perch on a mountain peak, however, the soul begins to see itself from a new perspective. The soul sees the world with a wider view.

Mountains are one of the soul's favorite hangouts because when one stands on a mountain, the soul expands. Of course, until the soul is acclimated to these new heights, it can be light-headed and somewhat dizzy. However, when the soul has adjusted to these new heights, she soars to a space of gratitude. Transfigured, soul's face takes on a glow of youthful radiance. Transformed, soul is ready to go even deeper into the experience of life.

Celtic spirituality describes such places as this as "thin places." Not only is the air thin, but on a mountain, as Edward Sellner points out, "a person experiences only a very thin divide between past, present, and future times." The experience of the disciples on the Mountain of Transfiguration seems to confirm how new altitudes can yield a new attitude toward life. This mountain was certainly one of those "thin places" where the dividing line between the past — as represented in the figures of Moses and Elijah, symbols of the law and the prophets — eases into the present as they heard the voice proclaiming Jesus to be the Beloved Son on whom God's favor rests. There was a very thin line in this very thin air of the mountain. The line between the present and the future grew even thinner as Jesus laid his hands on his friends and said, "Get up! Do not be afraid" (Matthew 17: 7). It was time to go. This dividing line seemed to dissolve as Jesus told his friends to keep this vision a secret until the Son would rise from the dead, adding a comment about his immanent passion and death. The thin line between life and death. The thin line between death and life.

In the thin air of this mountaintop experience, we see the thin line between transfiguration and transformation. Transfiguration occurs at the peak of the mountain. Transformation begins when one descends the mountain into the valley below. The temptation, as Peter suggested to Jesus at the end of the experience, is to want to stay on the mountain, to set up camp, to live forever in this thin air that makes one light-headed and lighthearted. However, the work of transformation occurs when we muster the courage to walk through the valley where death lingers in the shadows of every turn, where disagreements arise with those with whom we walk, where barricades of hostility and hatred block our path, where suffering and shame stalk our every step. Here the thin line between transfiguration and transformation may seem very thick indeed — so thick that it impedes our view of the mountain and makes the vision of glory fade.

In moments like this when the air is heavy and the mountain seems a distant memory, recall those words the disciples heard on the sacred summit: "This is my beloved Son on whom my favor rests." These are words that rain down from the mountain to the valley below. They are the words that reflect how God's favor rests on us — not just in our peak experiences but even in those moments when the bottom has fallen out.

Peter recalled these words and the vision he saw on the mountain in his second letter. He described himself as an eyewitness to God's majesty (2 Peter 1: 16). Then he added: "You will do well to pay attention to this as to a lamp shining in a dark place, until the day dawns and the morning star rises in your hearts (v. 19). With this admonition to pay attention to the vision, Peter has crossed the very thin line between transfiguration and transformation. Peter saw Jesus transfigured on the mountain, but Peter was transformed only by walking through the valley of death.

The morning my friend and I left the mountains, thick, gray clouds hung low over the snow-capped peaks. They were not the white, fluffy kind of clouds that seem so kind, that move so gently and playfully across the bright blue sky. These clouds seemed close to tears, and yet their anger or their pain remained out of our reach. The sun tried to change their mood, but was left hidden behind the shroud. Yet the gray clouds did not diminish the beauty of the mountains in the morning. They remained strong, confident in their sense of place. Mountains shall not be moved.

On our journey of conversion, we take some inspiration from those mountaintop experiences in our lives. When we are weak, the image of the mountain offers strength. When we are strong, the mountain reminds us how small we are and teaches us humility. When we are fearful, the memory of the mountain's song, "Do not be afraid," resounds in our hearts. And when we are downcast as we walk through the valley, as downcast as those clouds on the morning my friend and I left, the mountain reminds us that this too shall pass.

For pilgrims on the path of transformation, the metaphor of the mountain and the vision it reflects from its lofty peaks is an essential one. The image teaches us that even though we will never forget the glimpse of God's love on the mountain, it is only when we leave the peak that the work of transformation begins.

And it never really ends.

Story: The Mountain I See

The importance of keeping this transformation vision etched upon our hearts as we journey in life is reflected in this story about a young man named Brandon and his excellent adventure:

Brandon kept waking up the night before his big adventure. He'd sleep for an hour or so and then wake up and look at his alarm clock, certain that it wasn't working properly. Now he saw it was only two o'clock in the morning, and he had three more hours before the alarm would go off. So he tried to go back to sleep. Yet his eyes seemed glued to the hands of time illuminated in the darkness. His ears were attuned to the sound of the alarm. Just in case, he had even set his clock radio on the dresser to the station that played heavy metal music — with the volume turned up. He figured that even if he slept through the alarm, the rock music would roll him out of bed.

When the alarm did go off at five o'clock, Brandon was ready. He showered and finished packing his knapsack. Before closing the latch, he checked the list his grandfather had given him:

> Alarm clock — check.
> Map of the mountain — check.
> Flashlight — check.

Brandon's excellent adventure was about to begin. He stood on the porch and waited for his grandfather to drive up in his battered Chevy pickup. Brandon looked at his watch. Six o'clock. His grandfather should be here any minute, he thought; because his grandpa was always punctual. He paced on the front porch, glancing every now and then down the road. 6:15. No grandpa. By 6:30, Brandon was staring at the road certain that by the force of his gaze and concentration, his grandfather's truck would materialize. At seven o'clock, Brandon went into the kitchen to call. No answer. Now he was worried. What if his grand-father was sick or had an accident? By 7:30 Brandon couldn't wait any longer. His mom and dad were away for the weekend to see his sister and her new baby in California. When he dropped them off at the airport the day before, they told him he should only use the car in case of an emergency. Grandpa was an hour an a half late. This was an emergency. He got in the car and started driving to his grandfather's house.

On the way, he thought about the stories his grandfather had told him about the mountain. Brandon remembered his grandpa saying to him when he was little, "That mountain holds all the secrets of life. One day when you are older, I'll take you there. But you have to be ready or else you won't understand the secrets the mountain seeks to teach us."

In preparing for the trip, Brandon had asked his grandfather about the alarm clock, map and flashlight he had given to him.

"The alarm clock is more symbolic than practical," his grandfather said. "It's meant to remind you to stay awake so you can take in all the beauty the mountain holds. If you take a nap on the mountain, you'll miss its majesty and mystery. When we're on the mountain, we have to be wide awake to absorb into our body and soul the sights and sounds and smells of life that call the mountain home.

"As for the map, well, there are many paths on this mountain, paths worn by our ancestors who walked there before us. This map shows all the paths, and they are marked in such a way that we will know which ones to take and which ones to avoid in order to reach the top of the mountain. This map is our guide to tell us which way to go. Without it, we'd have a pretty fair chance of getting lost."

"And why the flashlight, grandfather?" Brandon had asked. It was a strange flashlight, not the kind you hold in your hand but the kind you strap to your forehead, like a miner's lamp.

"The flashlight will come in handy when we climb certain paths on the mountain. You see, some of these paths lead to the belly of the mountain, and if we want to explore these caves we'll need a light. It's important to strap the light to our forehead so our hands will be free.

Free to carry a walking stick — or free to grab hold of one another in case one of us falls."

When he arrived at his grandfather's house, the front door was open, but there was no sign of his grandpa. Brandon searched the house, the basement and the attic, and looked in the backyard and the garage, where he saw his grandfather's battered old Chevy truck. But no grandpa. He looked everywhere for a note that his grandfather might have left to explain what happened. There was no note. Then he noticed in the corner by the door that his grandfather's fishing poles were gone. It was the place where he always kept them. Brandon thought to himself, "I'll bet grandpa forgot all about our trip to the mountain and went fishing instead." He knew just where to find him — at the pond on the back forty. Sure enough, he found his grandfather sitting with his back to a tree, fishing.

"Grandfather," Brandon said somewhat breathlessly after running from the house to the pond. "Did you forget? We were going to the mountain today."

"Naw, I didn't forget," his grandfather said. Then, after a pause, "The fish are really biting this morning."

"I don't care about the fish! I wanted to go to the mountain. You promised you'd take me today."

"That I did, son," his grandfather said, "and you've just experienced the first lesson the mountain seeks to teach us."

Now Brandon was confused, and more than a little bit angry and frustrated. Sensing his frustration, his grandfather invited him to sit down beside him. "Look, Brandon, what do you see?"

Brandon looked around and saw all the usual things you'd see at a farm pond — water, trees, shrubs. "Wider, Brandon," his grandfather said. "Look wider. Expand your vision. What do you see?"

Far off in the distance, Brandon could see the mountain.

"There it is, Brandon. There's the mountain you're so anxious to climb. But it's not time yet. It's gonna be there a good long while. If you're too anxious to climb it, you'll be likely to miss its meaning. Take a good long look, Brandon. Stare at the mountain. Etch its image in your heart. That's where you have to see it first, or else you'll be blind to the wonders and wisdom it holds. Only when you know the mountain by heart will you be able to climb it. And when you know the mountain by heart, the mountain seems to bow, and comes to you."

From Brandon's perspective, spending the morning fishing instead of climbing the mountain was a not-so-excellent adventure. Still, this parable provides some of the important lessons to consider for the journey of transformation symbolized by that primary Scriptural metaphor, the mountain. On our adventure in the realm of God, Brandon's story and his grandfather's wisdom afford us an opportunity to get our bearings and check our equipment for this trip of transformation.

By Heart: The first lesson is to etch the vision upon one's heart. It is instructive to me that in the Roman Catholic lectionary the first reading for the first Sunday of the Church's year — the lectionary's first entry — is the vision of God's holy mountain from the prophet Isaiah (2: 1-5). It is the vision of the "mountain of the house of God" that "shall be established as the highest of the mountains, and shall be raised above the hills." This mountain becomes the sacred center, our ultimate destiny. It is the place where "all nations shall flow to it, and many peoples shall come." It is the sacred space where God teaches us the divine ways and where all human beings "walk in God's paths." This mountain becomes the learning center where God teaches us how to beat our swords into plowshares and our spears into pruning hooks. In this learning center, we unlearn the ways of the world: "neither shall they learn war any more."

Isaiah's image of God's holy mountain offers us the vision and beckons us to believe it as we sketch the image on our hearts. We are encouraged to know this vision by heart — not because it will come to pass in our lifetimes but because it is the vision of what will occur at the end of history. Isaiah doesn't oblige us to believe that a time will come when there will be no more wars on earth. History teaches us that for every sword hammered into a plowshare in one part of the world, somewhere else a pruning hook is being shaped into a spear. This doesn't mean we should accept war as a fact of life or, more accurately, a fact of death. Certainly we should do what we can to bring wars to an end. However, we should not hold onto a shallow optimism that will inevitably disappoint. Instead, we should hold to a deep, abiding hope by knowing Isaiah's vision of God's holy mountain by heart and by directing all that we are and all that we do into living that vision in our work, our relationships, our prayer, our attitudes, our actions.

Staying Awake: This brings us to a second important lesson carried in Brandon's adventure. It's about time. The story began with Brandon watching the clock, waiting for the alarm, prepared and ready to go. He was wide awake and full of anticipation, but his grandfather never showed.

Like Brandon anticipating his grandfather's arrival, we might want to carry an alarm clock as a symbol of our willingness to stay awake, stay alert, stay ready. We are living on God's time, which is always borrowed time. Borrowed time, however, is blessed time because it keeps us prepared. In borrowed time we don't take each other for granted. We don't take to telling lies, because someone living on borrowed time only has time for the truth.

Stephen Levine has phrased the question that goes along with this alarm clock: "If you only had one hour to live and could make only one call, who would it be to, what would you say, and why are you waiting?" This is transformation's wake-up call. It's about time to love, to forgive and to speak the truth we hear in our hearts.

The Map: The third lesson for mountain climbers and pilgrims on the journey of transformation is found in the map we carry with us. As Brandon's grandfather reminded him, the map to God's holy mountain shows us the many paths to peace.

I once saw a bumper sticker which read: "Give me a map and I'm magic." For Christian travelers on the transformation road to God's holy mountain, the map and the magic are found in the life of Jesus. Like Moses, who received the law of the covenant from God on a mountain, Jesus went to a mountain to deliver his most famous sermon that serves as the map on this mystical journey of transformation. In Matthew's Gospel, Jesus' Sermon on the Mount comprises three chapters, beginning with Chapter 5, verse 1: "Seeing the crowds, he went up on the mountain, and when he sat down his disciples came to him." It concludes with the last line of Chapter 7: "And when Jesus finished these sayings, the crowds were astonished at his teaching, for he taught them as one who had authority, and not as their scribes (vv. 28-29)." The effect of Jesus' spellbinding teaching that spelled out the map of what it means to be a follower is seen in the first verse of Chapter 8: "When he came down from the mountain, great crowds followed him."

Those who follow Jesus have their map to the mountain envisioned by Isaiah where the process of transformation will be complete. It is found in these three chapters from Matthew's Gospel in which Jesus "goes up on the mountain" to teach his disciples a new way of being. The first verses of this sermon that serves as our road map are the beatitudes — attitudes of being that provide a way of being with oneself, with God, with others and with all of creation. We see again how the altitude of a mountain changes attitudes and perceptions. The Beatitudes offer a unique perspective of being in the world. They provide a radical way of living that affects the way we look at ourselves and how we relate to each other in all areas of our lives. The map to the mountain offered by Jesus demands an attitude adjustment: from bad attitudes about ourselves, others and our world to *be*-attitudes — attitudes of being that are seen most clearly in actions of love and compassion in the service of God and others.

For example, the first beatitude, "Blessed are the poor in spirit, theirs is the kingdom of heaven," encourages us to cultivate the interior quality of spirit that embraces a vulnerability before our God. A healthy poverty of spirit implies dependence upon the kindness and compassion of God.

The be-attitude is this: We are all needy. Our very life depends on God. Deepening this attitude will lend itself to a spirit of humility, a lifestyle of simplicity and a very large heart of generosity. It is a poverty that shouts: "I am not alone!" An attitude that screams, "I need God! I need you! We need each other!" It is an attitude that answers the age-old question, "What's in it for me," with the response, "Nothing. Nothing is in it for me except the awareness that I am somebody in the eyes of God." Though we may be "nobodies" in the eyes of the world, because we are somebody in God's eyes we are more able to see something special in the eyes of others.

A true poverty of spirit will lend itself to an attitude of openness and trust in God. This is not a passive kind of dependence or a "Whatever will be, will be" attitude. Rather, it is a vigilant, visionary, expectant and active witness that all things and everything is possible because God is in charge.

The transformation that takes place when one embraces this attitude of being and converts it into an attitude of action, of doing, is tangible. The "me" generation becomes the "we" generation as we realize we are not alone, we need each other, depend upon each other and believe in the best in each other. A do-attitude unmasks the tough, "every one for himself or herself" with the tender truth that each one's pain, each one's loss, is a reflection of my own pain, my own loss.

A do-attitude of poverty in spirit counters the cultural maxim of self-sufficiency and consumerism with the Gospel truism that we are God-sufficient. We don't need more possessions, more property, more money to be seen as successful in the eyes of the world or to strengthen our sometimes shallow self-image because we are already made in the image of God, the image of self that is sacred in each of us. All that we are called to do is be faithful to that image presented in all its multifaceted and fascinating arrays in one another.

This be-attitude is played out in a do-attitude when we understand that hoarding things has a hollow ring, that independence is not freedom from but freedom to lend support, and that individualistic pursuits that lead one away from community are self-defeating and can only result in isolation. On the other hand, individualist gifts used in the service of others strengthens the bonds of our common life. These be-attitudes will lead us to deepen our commitment to the poor of our day, to challenge systems that institutionalize injustice or that profit from the absence of true peace.

The rest of the beatitudes which serve as the starting point on this mystical map to God's holy mountain call for the same kind of attitude adjustment. Jesus blesses those who are sorrowing, who are lowly, who hunger and thirst for holiness, who show mercy and are single-hearted, who make peace and who are persecuted for the sake of the reign of God.

This road map to God's holy mountain offered by Jesus in his Sermon on the Mount teaches that we don't have all the answers, but if we are willing to meet another in his or her need and get down on our knees to wash the feet of another, we might just catch a glimpse of the inheritance God has in mind for us. We shall inherit a land where treasures are buried beneath the feet of those we stop to greet along the way. We shall inherit a land of laughter and of tears where a sense of humor and a sense of the holy are not strangers but friends. It is a land where each one of us is valued not because of the power we wield or the fame we have found or the fortune we hold, but for the dignity that is our birthright, the dreams we embrace and our need for God.

As we follow this map, we seek always to share power rather than control others. We seek always to find the truth in another's position, no matter how distant or even distasteful the position seems to be. For we believe that beneath the lust for power, fame or fortune lies this truth: This one too is made in God's image.

When our commitment to living these be-attitudes into do-attitudes becomes a habit of our pilgrim hearts, the last beatitude reflects what will happen: Persecution is to be expected. When we seek to live counter to the culture by radically enfleshing these beatitudes, we will find around every corner not only the possibility but the probability of persecution. Because the culture is so enmeshed with principles contrary to the beatitudes, when we live in the way we have described here, we will know rejection and oppression.

So why do it? Why seek to incarnate these attitudes of being into actions of doing? Why bother to promote a new way of living and loving that embraces these attitudes of the heart? Why follow this map to God's holy mountain? We do it for the same reason that during World War II a German widow hid Jewish refugees in her home to protect them from Nazi death camps. She had her critics. In fact, her strongest criticism came from her neighbors when they discovered what she was doing. "You are risking your own well-being," they told her. "I know, I know," she said. "Then, why, why do you persist in this foolishness?" her neighbors demanded to know.

"I am doing it," the widow responded, "because the time is now, and I am here."

In the journey of transformation, memory and mercy are soul mates. We walk in the wisdom of that German widow. We learn from our mistakes. If we really understand and embrace the depth of God's love for us, if we feel in the fiber of our flesh and bones the power of the love expressed in the most dramatic example of God's mercy — the death and resurrection of Jesus — then we cannot help but make these attitudes of the heart into habits of our hearts. We will live in very human and very holy ways as we walk in solidarity to God's holy mountain.

Prayer: If we study the map of the soul, we won't lose our way. In order to read this map, however, we need a little light. Remember the flashlight Brandon's grandfather gave him for the trip to the mountain? It was a unique kind of light, attached by an elastic band to fit snugly around the head. As Brandon's grandfather pointed out, like miners exploring the caves of our hearts, prayer is the light that illuminates the path before us and the hope stored within us. Like that light strapped to our forehead, prayer becomes a third eye — the inner eye of wisdom and wonder. It calls us to look deep within and to recognize the face of the one who comes to meet us where we are.

Of course, the truth found in the primary incarnation story is that God doesn't meet us halfway on this journey. God comes down the mountain all the way, to be born in the midst of the mess of our lives.

As Brandon's grandfather reminded him, placing this light on our heads frees our hands to reach out to others along the way. With this lamp of prayer shining in the darkness, showing us the way, we'll be less likely to stumble. Yet even if we do, with empty hands stretched out in love, there will be someone there to catch us when we fall.

The alarm clock, map and miner's light are essential equipment for pilgrims who aspire to climb God's holy mountain. These symbols advise us that transformation is an ongoing process. Though our grandfather God may seem to be late, don't worry. Just be ready. Even if we rush off and go looking for God — and my guess is we'll find God fishing or wishing to teach us a little bit more about that mountain we so desperately seek — our hope is not about looking for God. Our hope is based on our belief that God is always on the lookout for us.

Incarnation stories reflect our belief in a God who came down to earth to walk this trail of transformation with us. In the next chapter we will turn to stories of redemption which remind us why God desires to walk with us on this road of life: to save us from our sin. Stories of redemption take place not on mountaintops where the view is beautiful to behold but in the valleys where the shadow of death stalks our path. It is here in the valley of death where we need to remember the glimpse of glory, the vision of abundant life, that the view from the mountain has provided. Now, however, we must move on through the valley to a lonely hill outside of the holy city. This is God's lookout point. It is the point where our redemption story is written not in words but in water and in blood.

GOD SAVES THE PEOPLE

Chapter Eight

Today salvation has come to this house.
— Luke 19: 8

Until one is committed, there is hesitancy, the chance to draw back, always ineffectiveness . . . . The moment one definitely commits oneself, then Providence moves, too. All sorts of things occur to help one that would never otherwise have occurred . . . . Boldness has genius, power, and magic in it. Begin it now.

— Johann Wolfgang van Goethe

Redemption stories underscore the point that God is always looking for an opportunity to save us. This is, after all, God's purpose in coming down the mountain to meet us where we are by being born in human likeness: to save us from sin and death.

To set the stage in the rest stops of the soul where our redemption stories are produced, imagine that we are children playing down by the creek that runs on the very edge of our property. It is early spring, a warm and wondrous day after a long and cruel winter. We are playing with our very best friend and having such a good time that when our mother calls us to come to the house for dinner we pretend that we don't hear her. We want to play just a little longer with this friend of ours, making believe that we are pirates in pursuit of a buried treasure or cowboys holding a fort or forty-niners in search of gold. Our mother calls again, but we keep on playing.

Then we hear a sound that we've never heard before. It sounds like thunder, but it's not coming from the sky. We remember how our mother has warned us that sometimes in the spring, when the weather grows warm, this little creek which is only a trickle can become a rushing stream. She had told us this more than once: Don't play near the creek in the early spring because the water comes with such a force that the current could take you away.

We begin to climb out of the creek bed to higher ground, but it's too late. The water is racing and raging down like a semi in a turnpike tunnel. We grasp for each other and then for a bush or a stump or solid ground as the water pours over us. Against the sound of the roaring waters, we hear our mother's voice calling us again. This time, however, she is closer, and when we look up she is standing on the bank, holding out a large branch and telling us to hold on tightly. We never knew how strong our mother was until that day as she pulls us out of certain death to safety on dry land. What surprises us even more than her strength is the tenderness of her embrace. She does not scold us for not heeding her warning; she does not reprimand us for playing too long and not listening to her when she called; she only puts her arms around us and says, "It's alright. You're safe now."

After holding us close to her, she says, "Let's go home. It's time for supper."

Our salvation story says we are like children who keep on playing and pretend not to hear God's voice when we are called. Like children absorbed in make-believe, we play our childish games.

Instead of being hurt by our lack of attention to the divine call, God decides to play along. God comes to us. At just the right time, in just the nick of time, God comes to hold out a branch that will never break, a plank of wood for us to grasp, and pulls us from our dangerous game of certain death to catch our breath.

This is the way our God comes so that we may believe and be saved. At the rest stops of the soul on the trail of transformation, these redemption stories remind us how God is looking after us. This divine vigilance to the human condition is seen in the way Jesus is always on the lookout for those who are in need. Throughout God's novel there are numerous tales of redemption, with Luke's Gospel especially focusing on this aspect of divine attentiveness to wayward children. For example, in Luke 19: 1-10 we read a redemption story of a man who is small in stature. This man, Zacchaeus, is not up a creek, but he is up a tree.

A Redemption Story: "Shorty" in the Sycamore Tree

The story goes that as Jesus is walking along the road one day, he makes a rest stop under a sycamore tree. As he is sitting there, someone asks him, "Rabbi, do you believe in luck?"

"Certainly," Jesus says with a twinkle in his eye. "How else can you explain the success of people you don't like?"

Then, as the story goes, he looks up and sees Zacchaeus perched like a bird on the branch of the sycamore tree. Most of the people surrounding Jesus that day know this man they had nicknamed "Shorty." And most of them don't like him at all. Indeed, their rallying cry whenever they see Zacchaeus, a successful businessman, is "Get Shorty!"

Is it luck or grace, curiosity or conviction, or — because of his reputation — simply seeking an avenue of escape that caused Zacchaeus to climb that tree? Zacchaeus is a tax collector, the chief tax collector, the Gospel says, which indicates that he is held in high esteem by his employers, the Romans. His livelihood has made him a wealthy man. But his privileged position in the eyes of the state places him outside the circle of his faith community. He is not only excluded by his own people because of what he does for a living, he is despised. He is viewed as a traitor because he has sold himself to the Roman occupation, for which he is well paid.

Even though he has sold his body by standing with the oppressors, and though he has sold his mind by using his financial skills to collect taxes, he has not yet sold his soul. This is evident by his strong desire to see Jesus. However, being "short in stature," in order to get a good look at this rabbi who is causing such a commotion and creating such a following, the little man with the large soul climbs a sycamore tree. Because Jesus, like his Divine Parent, is always on the lookout, he sees Zacchaeus. And because Zacchaeus' soul is ripe for picking, Jesus plucks this little man perched in a tree and invites him to be his host for the evening meal. From his rest stop under the sycamore tree, the next stop on Jesus' journey of the soul would be the home of a small man with deep pockets who is held in low esteem by those whose pockets were empty.

When Jesus enters this rest stop of Zacchaeus' house that night, the reign of God breaks through too. The tax collector who is guilty of extortion — taking money from his own people and giving it to the Romans — promises to repay all that he has taken, and more. Hearing the murmurs of the crowd who can't believe the rabbi would stoop so low as to dine with someone they have demonized, Zacchaeus says to Jesus: "Behold, Lord, half of my goods I give to the poor; and if I have defrauded any one of anything, I restore it fourfold" (Luke 19: 8). Realizing this payment is more than the letter of the law requires, Jesus responds, "Today salvation has come to this house" (v. 9).

The reason Jesus went to Zacchaeus' house that evening and spent time at this rest stop is the same reason why Jesus came into the world: "To seek out and to save the lost" (v. 10). Luke's Gospel, with its parables about the lost sheep, the lost son and the lost coin, points to this essential mission for which Jesus is responsible. One of the central ingredients in this mission of saving lost causes is sitting at the table with those who are identified as outcasts: people like Zacchaeus, people living "outside the law."

Because of the numerous references in the Gospels — from parables to proclamations about the coming of the reign of God to prophetic passages — Scripture scholars tend to agree that the Jesus of history spent much of his time breaking bread in "bad" company. Jesus felt more comfortable with outlaws. He broke down barriers by putting food between himself and the outcasts of the day. Jesus accepted their hospitality and so invited himself into their lives.

Remembering these redemption stories confronts us with the reality of Jesus' radical approach to relationships. Jesus was most comfortable with the outcasts, the poor, the broken, the shunned, the shamed. He broke bread with them, listened to their stories of struggle, poured some wine, and by his gentle presence and compassionate conversation reminded them of God's mercy.

ON THE LOOKOUT

The redemption story of Zacchaeus affords us an opportunity to look closely at our attitudes toward those we deem the "outcasts" of our day. A first step toward the reconciliation we find in our redemption stories, a reconciliation that leads to transformation, is to be on the lookout for the love of God in our lives. For we never know when God might surprise us and bring salvation to our house.

One day a couple of years ago when I was giving a retreat, a young man asked me to go with him to the state facility for girls who had been classified as juvenile offenders. He worked as a counselor there. Since the girls were unable to attend the retreat, he had arranged for those who wanted to come to an informal session where we could just talk. I met five or six teenage girls who, instead of making plans for the prom, were pondering how much time they had left in what they called prison. These were children of the night, kids from the street.

Yet, after spending a couple of hours in their company, I could see in each of them an imperishable spirit. One of them — her name was "Angel," though she called herself a "fallen one" — said this: "You know, I've been looking for God for a long time, looking behind doors, praying. But I'm frustrated. God doesn't seem to be around. Maybe I should just stop looking and let God find me."

I found wisdom in some street saints that day. Taken into custody and put away because of their poor choices and the chaos that had become their lives, these girls still bear within them the immortal spirit and unmistakable presence of God. One day this spirit that beats within them will surface, and they will embrace it and live it. This imperishable spirit will offer them a future.

On the ride back to the rectory, the young man who counsels these young girls, listens to them and challenges them, told me a bit more about Angel's story. She never knew her father, and her mother is also in prison in another state. As the young man talked, I could hear his deep concern and his wide compassion for Angel and the other girls. Day after day, he would go to their house and break bread with them, listen to their stories, encourage them to believe. Angel, who has been on the lookout for a long time for God, may not be able as yet to experience the measure of redemption and the moment of reconciliation she so desperately desires. But maybe one day, while talking with this counselor and sensing his compassion, she may be surprised by God's mercy even when she isn't looking.

Widen the Circle

Redemption stories challenge us to be watchmen and watchwomen who realize that within each person is a child of God — a child sometimes wounded but always full of wonder. To be on the lookout means believing that inside each of us there's a dream ready to be born. To be on the lookout demonstrates a trust that beneath the appearance, the masks, the frozen smiles and dirty faces there is an immortal spirit that is the image of God.

Jesus had the remarkable gift to see: to look beyond the sin and embrace the sinner, to see beneath the mask and uncover the dignity and the dream, to unravel the mess of misguided actions and bad breaks and revive that holy spirit that beats within every human heart.

There's a little of Zacchaeus and Angel in each of us. I recall a woman once saying to me after a retreat, "Like Zacchaeus, I'm small in stature; like Zacchaeus, I'm up a tree; but like Zacchaeus, I'll climb down one day." We too feel small at times, stained by sin or shame. We too are invited to "climb down" from our perches, pedestals and penthouses to accept the invitation of Jesus to follow the way of forgiveness. This is the path that leads to transformation.

This quality of mercy is revealed in our willingness to share our stories and listen to the stories of others as Jesus was willing to listen to Zacchaeus, as the young man was willing to share Angel's story of loneliness and pain. This is one way that salvation comes to our house: By following the example of Jesus and that young man, we break through the barriers others impose and welcome into our hearts those who have been cast out.

When we invite Jesus to our house as a guest, in whatever disguise he may be employing that day, we welcome salvation. All that is required of us is that we accept Jesus' invitation to be his companion at the table and that we receive God's mercy for any injustice we may have done or any justice we may have failed to do. With Jesus' gesture of going to the house of Zacchaeus, the great circle of God's forgiveness remains unbroken and even expands to include the least likely suspects in salvation's story.

This is our hope at this rest stop of redemption: that someday, when we are feeling small because our sin is so large, someone will pass along the way and say, "I intend to dine at your house tonight" (Luke 19: 5).

We will reply, "You are most welcome, friend, but know that my house is a mess." The friend in turn will say, "I know. Why do you think I want to come to your house for dinner?"

CHERISH: A REDEMPTION STORY

Here is another modern-day myth drawn from the experience of the little man who was up a tree.

"Easy" was not her name, it was her occupation. But to understand how she came to spend her nights on the dimly lit street corners and in a broken-down boarding house, one must untangle the web of her life's story.

When she was born, her mother gave her the name Cherish. It was an unusual name, but her mother wanted her to know that from the moment of her birth she was a precious gift. Her father deserted her mother when she wouldn't have an abortion. So Cherish was raised by her mother and didn't know who her father was. When she was growing up and began to recognize that her home was different from those of other children she played with, she would ask her mom about her father. Her mother would cradle Cherish close to her breast and say simply, "Don't worry, dear, I'm never going to leave you." She never answered her daughter's question, nor did she keep her promise.

Cherish's mother died when she was ten, and Cherish was sent to a home where girls of all ages shared one thing in common: They were alone.

On the grounds of her new home, there was a large maple tree with a wooden platform nestled in its branches. Cherish often climbed the tree and sat for hours in the loneliness of its limbs. She often cried, confused and angry that her mother had left her. The only person who ever loved her or she ever loved would never again caress her fragile body. In between the tears, however, Cherish would dream. She saw faraway places with people who smiled and laughed. She dreamed of one person in particular, her knight in shining armor who would take Cherish in his arms and take away her pain. He would show her once again how to love and be loved, how to care and be cared for, how to forgive and be forgiven.

Cherish spent six years at that home. Then one night, after a few moments in her favorite hiding place in the maple tree, as the moon danced on the branches, Cherish decided to run away. She didn't know where she was going, but she knew she couldn't stay there waiting for that special person to come and make her dream come true. She had to go and search for him.

She walked for hours along a lonely stretch of country road. Finally someone stopped. A nice enough man, she thought at first, but before the night was over he would use her body for his pleasure and leave her in a ditch, her clothes torn and tattered, her body bruised and bleeding.

Cherish had begun her tragic journey into the dark side of life. She spent the next five years selling the only thing she had, her body, to men who paid her well. She always had enough work. Yet she still dreamed. Since there were no treehouses in the city, she sat in darkened doorways or in silent cafes at closing time, smoking cigarettes and imagining that out of the smoke a genie would appear to take her home.

One night, as she sat alone in the last booth of Al's All-Night Diner, a young man in his mid-twenties came and sat down across from her. Cherish was tired and told him to get lost. But he stayed. He bought her a cup of coffee and talked about the weather and the win by the Cardinals that day. Cherish was attracted by his voice. It was not rough and raspy like so many of the men she met. This one was different somehow from the others she met in her work. They talked through five cups of coffee and two pieces of Al's apple pie.

At last he spoke the words she dreaded to hear: "I want to take you to my place." Though she thought he was different, he was just like all the rest. Another john. But she needed the money and took his hand.

At the counter, the old men who knew Cherish murmured, "There goes Easy with another one." And they chuckled as they remembered. When they got outside, the young man suggested that they go to Cherish's place instead. "Probably has a wife and kids at his place," Cherish thought to herself.

When they came to the small room above the bakery that Cherish called home, she asked for the money up front. The young man looked at her, and a gentle smile creased his face. There was tenderness in his voice as he said, "That's not why I'm here. Can we just talk? I want to get to know you better."

So that night, instead of Cherish sharing her bed, she shared her story. At dawn, the young man left, taking with him some of her pain.

Cherish watched him as he crossed the street below. From this view above the bakery, she thought back to that treehouse of long ago and believed once again that maybe dreams do come true.

Like Zacchaeus and Angel, Cherish found some redemption in just being able to share her story. Cherish, who had been on the lookout for a long time for that one person to come and take her pain away, experienced a measure of redemption and a moment of reconciliation when she wasn't looking. Like Jesus, the young man was willing to share Cherish's story of loneliness and pain without expectations of receiving something in return. Nor did he expect that by spending a few hours with her he would solve her problems. The story suggests something about how salvation comes to our house: We can't fix all the world's problems; we can't fix all our own problems; we can't fix the brokenness in other's lives; we can't fix the hurt in some relationships. No matter how gifted we are, there are some realities in life that are beyond our control.

What we can do, however, is to be open to those problems, that brokenness, that hurt by following the example of Jesus. Travelers on the road of transformation are always on the lookout, always ready to stop and listen to a story, always willing to make some time, some space, to hold another's hurt and help another cry.

Our Most Grievous Wound

But sometimes the wound inflicted by our sin is so great, so deep, that it may take years to allow it to heal. Recently, a woman shared with me a very powerful story of her own conversion to believe in the power of God's — and her own — forgiveness.

When she was nineteen, within a month of the Supreme Court decision that legalized abortion, she found herself unwed and pregnant. When the doctor told her that abortion was now legal, she accepted his offer to end this pregnancy in a very quick and efficient way.

She experienced some remorse and confessed her sin at the time, and the priest assured her she was forgiven and that she should "get on with her life." Just as she had accepted the doctor's offer of an abortion, she accepted the priest's absolution and went on with her life. But accepting God's forgiveness is one thing; far more difficult, she said, is forgiving oneself.

Fourteen years went by before God gently took this woman by the hand and said that the time had come for her to find healing from her abortion. "Peace can only come from looking back at those dark, painful areas of our lives that haunt us," she told me, "but God always sends someone to help us along that dark path." She then began the slow, anguishing journey of bringing her past to light. As she did, she began to find healing.

Part of this journey of healing involved helping others. She became aware of a gentle call from God to help some other women find healing from the experience of abortion. Reaching out to someone else meant sharing her past. She was terrified to do so because of what others might say if they knew she had done something so dreadful. But God kept chipping away at her fears until finally one day she made this deal with God: "I will cheerfully minister to post-abortion victims if you send me someone who needs my help."

Well, it's dangerous to make deals with God because God always makes good on God's part of the bargain. One day, a friend confessed to her that she had had an abortion. This friend's confession brought the woman to the threshold of transformation. Then another shared her story with this woman, and she inched ever closer to telling her own story. One day, when she mustered the courage to share her own story with her closest friend, she found out that, on the day before, this friend had confessed her own experience of abortion. For the first time, after twenty-eight years, the friend had spoken of an abortion she had had when she was in her early twenties.

The woman told me that "too many men and women live in fear of confessing their sins and seeking reconciliation." But she believes God chose to take her back to a very dark period in her life and to use her healing as an avenue of hope to others in great pain.

Vulnerability is a key factor in widening the circle of compassion and setting the table for our continuing conversion in grace. As soon as one opens one's mouth and speaks from one's heart, one is vulnerable. One doesn't know how the other will respond. To be transformed, however, we must be willing to take a few risks: to climb down the tree as Zacchaeus did, to share our story with a stranger as Cherish did, to speak our own truth as this woman did. Reconciliation will remain a distant dream and mercy will only be a mirage if we allow our most grievous wounds, whether they are self-inflicted or inflicted upon us by others, to fester within us.

THE VULNERABILITY OF JESUS

We sense his ability to be vulnerable in the life of Jesus. Though divine, Jesus was also fully human. The humanity of Jesus is seen most clearly in those instances of great vulnerability. The clearest example, of course, is the cross. Stripped of everything from clothes to companionship, the tortured, naked body of Jesus as he hangs on the cross is a powerful image of the kind of vulnerability that leads to the victory of reconciliation and redemption. Even after his resurrection, Jesus was not afraid to show his wounds. The ability to expose one's wounds seems a necessary ingredient in the process of reconciliation.

Even before his crucifixion and resurrection, however, Jesus often brought people near by taking away the barriers that kept them apart. This was not just a spiritual exercise but a physical one. There was something very physical about Jesus. He was not afraid to touch others. When we consider the many miracle stories that reveal the inbreaking of God's reign of redemption, there is an extraordinary emphasis on Jesus' physical presence. He literally touched people and restored them to wholeness. Remember Jesus spitting and touching the deaf mute's tongue, or making a mud pack to put over the eyes of the blind man. He touched them and they came to their senses again. People with an assortment of physical disabilities and spiritual maladies experienced a breakthrough when Jesus touched them: His healing touch broke through their diseases of body and spirit to bring them closer to the reign of God.

As much as he touched others, Jesus also allowed himself to be touched. Recall the poignant story in John's Gospel when, just a week or so before his death, Jesus went to Bethany to visit his old friends, Lazarus, whom he had raised from the dead, and his two sisters, Martha and Mary. True to their personality types captured in Luke's famous story of these two sisters, Martha prepared and served supper while "Mary took a pound of costly ointment of pure nard and anointed the feet of Jesus and wiped his feet with her hair" (John 12: 3). Jesus, tired from walking the dusty roads, his feet throbbing from standing all day to teach and to heal, found comfort in this gentle, intimate gesture.

Here we see how vulnerable Jesus was able to be. He "put his feet up" and relaxed. His journey was about to end in Jerusalem. His walking days were numbered as he neared his final earthly destination. So Jesus now allowed Mary to anoint his tired and aching feet. It was an act of reverence.

Reflexologists believe the healing of one's body and the release of tension can happen by touching certain spots on a person's feet. As we walk this road of transformation, we may want to make an appointment with a reflexologist or a massage therapist. Jesus did. Mary massaged Jesus' feet with the expensive oil whose fragrance filled the house.

The scene reflects a sacred vulnerability. Jesus was not afraid to be touched. He was not afraid to have Mary's hair lightly brush across his feet. This was a moment of pleasure before the pain. Mary attended to the needs of Jesus. In an act of love and holy service, she anointed his feet just a few days before he would be abandoned. It was a memory Jesus could cling to in his darkest hour when his body would be bruised and cut with whips of violence. He would be stripped, and standing naked before his accusers, his body would be mocked. People would seek to shame him, would ridicule his nakedness, would laugh as strips of jagged, sharp metal sliced through the very skin that Mary had anointed with tenderness.

During this ugly ordeal, as he stood naked before those who violently attacked him, Jesus would remember something his favorite prophet, Isaiah, wrote: "God helps me . . . and I know I shall not be put to shame" (Isaiah 50: 7). But he would also remember Mary's gentle touch. He implies this as he says to those who were so concerned about the cost of the perfume: "Leave her alone, let her keep (the oil) for the day of my burial" (John 12: 7).

At this rest stop in Bethany at the home of old friends, Jesus says there can be no "waste" in the cause of love. When one is in love, there is no price so high, so exorbitant, that one wouldn't pay. In love's service no price is too high. The fragrance of Mary's act of love filled the house and filled Jesus' soul.

To reasonable folks like Judas, who complained that the money used to purchase this expensive perfume could instead have been used for the poor, this was a senseless act. Of course it was. A senseless act of beauty, of compassion, of kindness. From the bottom-line perspective of financial accountability, it was a waste of money. It didn't make any sense. But from the soulful perspective of redemptive vulnerability, it made perfect sense.

Mary was in the service of love that day, and she would not be denied. This scene in John's Gospel of Mary anointing the feet of Jesus is not unlike the scene in Luke's Gospel when she spent the day at the feet of Jesus, hanging on his every word while her sister, Martha, was busy about the details of hospitality. From these stories, we might get the impression that Mary lacked common sense. After all, common sense would have told her to help her sister in the kitchen. Common sense would have taught her not to spend so much money on perfume.

Remember, however, that this expedition on the highway of holiness is not a journey of the head but of the heart and soul. The common sense approach of budgets and bottom lines is thrown out the window as the soul's uncommon sense shows us the way. That is why travelers on the trail of transformation have that familiar bumpersticker slogan inviting people to "practice random acts of kindness and senseless acts of beauty." Mary of Bethany is a patron saint of this kind of "uncommon sense" approach to life. By sitting at the feet of Jesus, absorbing his every word, she learned the uncommon sense of Jesus that allowed him to be fully awake, fully present to those he encountered along the way. Her lavish act of love in anointing Jesus' feet was a reflection of his uncommon outpouring of love into her life and into the world.

By practicing random, redemptive acts of kindness and senseless, sacred acts of beauty, we become fully awake to the mystery of the divine presence in our lives. We allow all our uncommon senses to be open so as to see the friend hidden in the stranger, taste and savor the fresh-baked bread of life, hear the whispers of those outside the walls of our comfortable communities, touch the festering wounds of those who live in fear and anoint the feet of weary pilgrims lost in love as we smell the sweet fragrance of God's forgiveness.

COMING TO OUR SENSES

To help us experience this aroma of God's mercy, we recall a familiar redemption story, the Prodigal Son (Luke 15: 11-32). This parable's poetic edge points out how important our uncommon senses are.

Similar to what we heard in the Zacchaeus story, recall that Jesus tells the Prodigal Son parable amid murmurs and whispers: "This man receives sinners and eats with them" (Luke 15: 2). Surrounded by his friends — that marginal mob of tax collectors and known sinners (how interesting that these folks were famous for their sins since most of us are "unknown" sinners) — Jesus proceeded to tell this classic tale of love's forbearance and forgiveness. Though we have heard this story many times, I want to highlight a few phrases and invite us to hear them as if for the first time.

But when he came to himself (v. 17). The New American Bible translates this phrase as, "coming to his senses," which underscores the message about the uncommon sense we've been reflecting on here. However, the Revised Standard Version translation also illuminates the importance of the senses in the journey of a soul. The phrase "but when he came to himself" suggests how the younger son has been out of touch. When someone wakes up after being knocked out, we say, "He's coming to." The young man has squandered his inheritance on wine, women and song and now is destitute. He comes to himself by noticing how raw his hands are from laboring on the farm. He comes to realize how his stomach aches from hunger. He comes to see how his vision is blurred by his tears caused by the stench of the pigs. He comes to his senses and hears that tiny voice within him telling him to go home.

But while he was yet at a distance, his father saw him and had compassion (v. 20). The grieving father has been on the lookout, keeping watch, hoping that one day he would see his son coming down the road to the place where he belonged. Compassion fills the old man's heart at the sight of the young man staggering beneath the burden of shame and embarrassment. Can he see his son rehearsing the line that would acknowledge his sin and set the table for the feast of forgiveness? No, probably not, because the prodigal is "yet at a distance." But true to redemption's demand, the father is on guard duty, watching for his wayward son.

He ran and embraced him and kissed him (v. 20b). When the father sees his son coming down the road, he does not stand aloof, arms folded, waiting for the son to come to him. No, he races out to meet him with arms outstretched. And a handshake just won't do. This reunion calls for a kiss.

The father couldn't wait to see his son. His first impulse is not to punish the young man but to welcome him home. Though the boy has his confession speech, his act of contrition, ready and begins to utter it, the father will hear nothing of it. There is no "equal justice" here; no thought of "pay back every cent you owe and then we can think about taking your place in the family again." No, this father says, "Bring the best robe and put it on him; and put a ring on his hand, and shoes on his feet" (v. 22). (Dancing shoes, one would presume, because of the party planned for later in the evening.) "Bring the fatted calf and kill it, and let us eat and make merry; for this my son was dead, and is alive again; he was lost, and is found" (vv. 23-24).

In other words, the father says, "Spend more!"

The father's response is certainly not the common sense approach to life and relationships that most of us practice. It is difficult enough for me to forgive another who has taken from me, used me, betrayed me. Even if I could work up the courage to forgive, to shake hands, to start from scratch, the farthest thing from my mind would be to "kill the fatted calf."

So I know what the older brother must have felt. When he comes home after a long day of working in his father's fields and hears "music and dancing" (v. 25), and then discovers that his younger brother, the spoiled brat, is back and that there is a great party for him, well, the older brother goes into a rage. A righteous rage. He has a right to rage.

Or so it seems.

He stews outside for a while. He won't go inside the house. Just as he did for the younger son, however, the father comes out of the house to meet the older son on the son's own terms. He meets the raging son in his own place, a place of self-righteousness. The older brother proceeds to make his case. The forgiving father listens intently and with compassion as his firstborn lists the reasons why he has every right to feel the way he does.

The father understands his oldest son's position and does not deny his feelings. He doesn't say, "Don't feel that way." Instead, he gently puts the party in proper perspective. In this case, "proper" also means "God's perspective":

Son, you are always with me, and all that is mine is yours. It was fitting to make merry and be glad, for this your brother was dead, and is alive; he was lost, and is found (vv. 31-32).

Notice the phrase, "It was fitting." The implication is that they have no other choice but to celebrate the son's return. Oh, there are other choices — let the son grovel for a time, feel ashamed, work his way back into the family, punish him. These are choices many of us might make in similar situations.

But to throw a party? To take the prime rib out of the freezer — the one you've been saving for that special occasion — and invite all the neighbors and friends and relatives and treat this prodigal like a returning hero rather than a sinner? Would these gestures appear on our list of "things to do" with the prodigals of our lives? Would these be thought of as "fitting" responses for those of us who would rather exact a "pound of flesh" instead?

Uncommon Sense

At redemption's rest stop on the road of holiness, the old ways of resolving conflict are no longer useful because conversion implies becoming a new creation. As Paul writes, "If anyone is in Christ, he or she is a new creation; the old has passed away; behold, the new has come" (2 Corinthians 5: 17).

New robe. New ring for his finger. New leg of lamb for the feast. Yes, the forgiving father knew something about being a new person. Redemption stories like the Prodigal Son remind us that it is God who makes all things new. And in making all things new, God has given us, through Christ, "the message of reconciliation" (v. 18). This is the message that has been entrusted to us. Paul makes it very clear: God does not keep score. God does not "count our trespasses against us" (v. 19). No matter how large or small these transgressions are, God is the pardoning parent who runs out to meet us and welcome us home.

On the trail of transformation, then, our senses are opened and our uncommon sense is awakened. The old common sense found in the balance sheet of "an eye for an eye" that left people vision-impaired is now turned into a new insight: Spend more on forgiveness. Now, the uncommon sense found in the redemption story of the forgiving father's pardon of his prodigal son makes us, in Paul's phrase, "ambassadors for Christ" (v. 20). This is our new and uncommon role as we walk this trail of transformation with those who have hurt us or betrayed us or stolen from us: We are ambassadors of a new creation where reconciliation replaces revenge, where forgiveness overwhelms the fear of receiving pardon, where outstretched arms symbolize the ever-widening circle of mercy. When we practice this ministry of reconciliation found in our redemption stories within our relationships with those with whom we feel distant or estranged, we begin to develop our uncommon sense that will help us to be always on the lookout for the prodigals we meet along the way. Whether they are up a creek or down in the dumps, up a tree or down for the last count, we will run out to meet them with arms outstretched and will welcome them into the ever-expanding circle of redemption.

Wouldn't you agree that living in such a forgiving way just makes good sense?

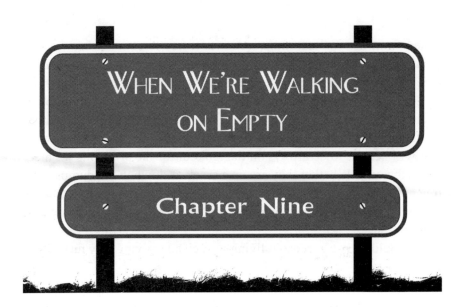

WHEN WE'RE WALKING
ON EMPTY

Chapter Nine

*Though he was in the form of God, Jesus did not count equality
with God a thing to be grasped, but rather emptied himself.*

– Philippians 2: 3-11

*It is a terrible thing
To be so open: it is as if my heart
Put on a face and walked into the world.*

– Sylvia Plath, "A Poem For Three Voices"

We have been walking on this road of transformation for a long time
now. We've made more than a few rest stops along the way, but perhaps
the journey has been so long that some of us are running on fumes. The
primary redemption story of the Christian tradition reminds us that
running out of gas is par for this course. We've come all this way to
learn that this is the point: We have to learn how to walk on empty.

Emptiness is not a condition most of us find very comfortable. We
usually want to fill the emptiness. When we receive the warning that
we are close to empty, we automatically reach for something to fill the
void. Empty stomachs growl, and we eat. When the warning light goes
on in the car indicating that we're almost out of gas, we look for a
service station to refuel. Empty hearts give a signal too. There's no
spring in the step. We have winter legs — legs that move slowly as if

we're plodding through a field of snow. Empty hearts are also reflected in the eyes: no light, no spark. When others see us, they wonder if anyone is at home.

When we're in such a state, we're in a good place to consider the primary redemption story of the Christian faith: the suffering, death and resurrection of Jesus. Christians make this journey every year in the spring. We call it Holy Week. This perilous pilgrimage filled with unimaginable pain and unexpected promise begins on Palm Sunday and stretches for seven days. On the seventh day, Easter Sunday, we arrive at our destination at that place which symbolizes the ultimate transformation that God envisions for humanity. It's holy irony that this place where we experience the eternal consequences of our conversion course is also empty: the empty tomb.

WALKING ON EMPTY

As we explore the nature of emptiness that leads to transformation, a memory surfaces for me. I learned to drive with a car that had standard transmission and more horsepower than I could possibly corral. One terrifying memory from this experience that is etched in my mind is sitting on the upslope of a hill, waiting for the light to change. "Go easy on the clutch," dad advised. But because I was having so much difficulty learning how to drive this car, I was convinced this was an evil clutch. There was a line of cars behind me filled with impatient drivers who wanted to get through the light before it changed to red. But I kept stalling out the car. We'd start rolling backwards. I'd slam on the brake. Try again. Kill the engine. Roll backwards. Slam the brakes. Try again. When I finally took off, the tires squealed and shot rocks and pieces of asphalt on the cars behind me. I made it through the light on yellow. I made a vow that day to never again drive a car with an evil clutch.

As we continued in traffic, I was so concerned with that clutch that nothing else seemed to matter. Like a mantra, my dad kept repeating, "Go easy on the clutch." But I pleaded: "Couldn't I take the test in mom's car?" Mom had a car with an automatic transmission.

We hit the open road. I felt free — no clutch to worry about. I thought, "Well, I can do this." We were driving to my grandparents' farm about an hour away. Dad decided to take a nap. No problem, Dad, I think I'm getting the hang of it. I should have said, "Could you not stay awake with me for one hour?" Fifteen minutes or so into Dad's nap, the car coughed a few times and came to a stop. This awakened my father. "What did you do now?" he asked.

"I didn't do anything," I said. "The car just stopped." At my dad's insistence, I kept turning the ignition. No response. All those horses under the hood were sound asleep. Dad got out of the car and opened the hood. Then he came to the driver's side of the car and motioned me to move over. He didn't bother turning the key in the ignition. He took one look at the gas gauge and said, "This 'E' does not stand for 'Excellent driver.'" I had been so preoccupied with that clutch that I never thought to look at the gas gauge. Then Dad said, "There's a gas can in the trunk. Start walking."

From a car with an evil clutch that was running on empty, I found myself with gas can in hand walking on empty. That's inevitably what we do when we wander the road of Holy Week: We walk on empty.

The redemption stories we hear during Holy Week remind us that it is only when we are walking on empty that God can show us the rest of the way. The journey begins with a song on our lips: the hymn from Paul's letter to the Philippians (2: 3-11) which reflects that our attitude must be the attitude of Christ. It is an attitude of emptiness: "though he was in the form of God, Jesus did not count equality with God a thing to be grasped, but rather emptied himself" (vv. 6-7). Jesus emptied himself until his emptiness was complete: death on a cross.

On Calvary, Jesus experienced the ultimate humiliation. He had to be empty in order to endure those who struck his back, plucked his beard and spit in his face. Though his persecutors insulted him and disgraced him, Jesus would not be put to shame. Like the suffering servant from the prophet Isaiah, his face became like flint. The insults, the beatings, the humiliation flew off him like sparks. Why? Because he was empty — empty enough to know it was God's presence within him that resisted the violence they were doing to him. He could not be put to shame because when they stripped him what was exposed was God.

EMPTY VESSELS

So, how do we learn to walk on empty? The same way I learned how to drive a car with an evil clutch: the hard way. Maybe my dad's mantra, "Go easy on the clutch," offers us another clue. When we are in the clutches of evil, go easy on ourselves. Empty ourselves. Allow God the room to resist the evil. For only when we empty ourselves can God be exposed. We hear it in the Philippians hymn: Because Jesus emptied himself, accepting even death on a cross, God raised him up.

When we've run out of fuel — the fuel of dreams, of hope, of compassion, of forgiveness — we learn how to walk on empty. Instead of carrying a gas can in hand, however, we carry another kind of container. We carry this container not in our hands, but in our hearts. It is shaped like a cup, and we notice the cup is empty.

Our prayer at the rest stops during this sacred sojourn empties this cup, this chalice of our hearts. Rather than fill our hearts, prayer purges our hearts. Meditating on the passion story of Jesus, we can sense how this happens.

At the very beginning of the story as told by Mark, Jesus is in Bethany. Unlike John, who placed Jesus at the home of old friends, in Mark's telling of this redemption story Jesus is at the house of Simon the Leper, an outcast. An unidentified woman carries a container that is full of perfume. She breaks the jar and pours the perfume on the head of Jesus. She empties the container to anoint the body of Christ. As in John's rendition of this episode, some call this act an extravagant waste of money. After all, this perfume might bring as much as 300 pieces of silver that could be given to the poor. The high cost of perfume is ten times the cost of a person: Jesus was betrayed for thirty pieces of silver. Jesus, however, will walk the rest of the way with the scent of this perfume of one who lovingly is emptying her heart to anoint his body for burial.

Later, as the disciples ask about preparing a room for the Passover feast, Jesus tells them to be on the lookout for a man carrying a water jar. Another vessel, this one filled with water. Follow him, Jesus says. Can we imagine this jar having a tiny crack in it, causing the water to leak out ever so slowly but leaving a trail? This trail leads to the room where Jesus will celebrate one last time in the company of his friends. The water jar, like our hearts at times, is broken. When our hearts are broken, hope leaks out and leaves a trail for another to find a place where he or she can find some company, some compassion.

When all hope leaks out of these broken hearts, these hearts become empty — and ready for God.

When Jesus and his disciples arrive for that meal, they see the room is spacious. There's more than enough room to gather with a few friends. Then we see another vessel, a cup filled with wine. Before he offers this cup to his friends to drink, Jesus knows his heart is already empty. One of these friends would betray him. Another would deny even knowing him. From this empty heart, Jesus offers the cup of a new covenant. Take and drink, he says. This is my blood. Taste it, drink deeply of it until the cup resembles the heart of Jesus: empty. The new covenant is found in a cup — a heart — that is poured out for friends, some of whom betray and deny his friendship.

Even later, after the meal, Jesus takes a few friends and invites them to join him in prayer. Once again, the image of a cup becomes the focus of his prayer: "Take this cup away from me." For these anguishing moments in the garden, Jesus feels the emptiness, the abandonment, the purgatory of his passion. The cup is empty, he prays. Take it away. There must be another way.

In the silence of that starless night, however, Jesus' prayer calls him to empty himself even more. In emptying himself completely, he will collect in his body, in his heart, all the pain and suffering, sin and death that the world has to offer.

These incidents from the passion story of Mark offer the challenge to become empty vessels that long to be filled with redemption. Meditation on the passion of Christ at these rest stops of the soul raises the question: What needs to be emptied in my life? At redemption's rest stop, we are asked to abandon ourselves, empty ourselves, of any ambition or intention that will try to fill the void we feel inside. The temptation will be to try to fill the emptiness. Yet we need to resist that temptation. We are challenged to stay with the emptiness. After all, there's nothing we can do to stop this execution. There's nothing we can do. This is emptiness; this is the prayer of abandonment.

We may want to say with Jesus, "Take this empty cup away. I don't want to be empty. I want to be filled." Only when we are empty, however, can we find true wisdom and a courage that is not our own. This emptying is total: all fear, all lies and, yes, all hope and all dreams. For this seven-day trip is about walking on empty — and being filled with the divine presence.

Only when the vessel of our heart is emptied of self, of our own personal ambitions and fear, can we be filled with God. And when we are filled with God, hope will spill out.

If we are faithful to this prayer quest by walking on empty, then we will discover that at the destination that defines our destiny the only thing that will be empty will be a tomb. An empty tomb.

REST STOPS: A SENSE OF PLACE

There are three rest stops where we rendezvous with redemption during the seven-day sojourn of Holy Week. They are connected by a sense of place. In our emptiness, we hear God's invitation: "I'll meet you there."

I'll meet you around a table to share stories of memory and hope.

I'll meet you at a cross to embrace your sorrow and shame, your sin and pain.

I'll meet you at an empty tomb to celebrate your joy and make real my promise of life.

God meets us at these places and pledges love and fidelity. These are the places, the rest stops, where God desires to meet us during the pilgrimage of Holy Week: at a table, at a cross, at an empty tomb. In these places we listen for the real presence of God in stories of ancestors escaping death — and a revolutionary rabbi who did not. We look for the real presence of God in bread broken and broken hearts. We taste the real presence of God in wine poured out as blood.

These are the places where God desires to meet us. The question is: Are we empty enough to give God some room to maneuver and find us?

The first rest stop is at a table. There's an empty place reserved for each of us, an empty place waiting to be filled. It's a place where we can see and be heard. It's a place where we can taste the sweet wine of compassion, the flavor of fidelity, even as we smell the foul odor of betrayal. It's a place where we can have our feet washed and our hands dried. No sweating palms tonight. No nervous laughter, only genuine joy — at least for a while. It will be awhile before we have to leave the table and walk with our clean feet to our next meeting place.

At this rest stop, we spend time remembering. This is the night we celebrate the Passover of our God. This night is about telling stories of our ancestors' flight to freedom and our own stories of liberation. This is the night when we learn how to stay at the table even when we know one of those with whom we have shared life and love will betray us. Another, perhaps our closest friend, will speak bold promises but before this night is over will deny even knowing us. We have much to learn at this rest stop: about knowing when to stay and when it's time to leave. Are we empty enough to listen and to learn?

This is the night when we take simple gifts of bread and wine into our empty hands and remember the promise and the instruction: "Whenever you do this — whenever you gather around a table in the company of friends; whenever you wash the feet of others in acts of holy service; whenever you tell the stories of your ancestors' adventures; whenever you pass the cup of blessing and sorrow, of triumph and tears, I will be there; remember me."

God says to us at this rest stop: "I know this place. I created this space. I'll meet you there."

We know such places, don't we?

I remember the kitchen table at Steve and Connie's house. They lived just down the street from the rectory in the first place where I practiced being a public minister. There were many nights during my deacon year when I would walk to their house, sit at their kitchen table and talk about the day, the week, the friends, the fear. We would munch on chips or nibble on cookies or cake, drink coke or coffee, and tell the stories that shaped our lives or were taking shape or were causing us to feel bent out of shape. During those months of getting my feet wet as a public minister, Steve and Connie washed my feet, my hopes, my dreams. At Connie and Steve's kitchen table, hope was nurtured and courage was gathered in the company of these friends.

We know such a place, such a table, don't we? The family table when all are home for dinner. The coffee table when a friend drops over for a visit. The picnic table in the backyard on a summer's evening. At this rest stop, we remember the places where people are seen and heard and understood. At such a table, in such a holy place, in the company of such friends, life is valued, faith is strengthened, stories are sacred and memory lives.

And God says, "I'll meet you there."

Earlier this year, I met Steve and Connie around the dining room table in the home of a mutual friend. Though I've seen Steve and Connie often in the sixteen years since we first met at their kitchen table, this was an evening that resurrected the memory. New stories of family, of struggles, of hope were told. We raised wine glasses to toast the covenant of our friendship. How much has happened in our lives since we first met. And how much remains the same: Whenever we gather in the company of friends to tell the stories of our faith and our fear, God says, "I'll meet you there." When we left that night, the wine glasses were empty but our hearts were full.

FINDING A PLACE AT THE TABLE

This rest stop of the soul is also about finding a place at the table of community when we've been hurt or betrayed, pushed away or told we don't belong. Once I met an elderly gentleman, whom I'll call Herman, who came up to me with tears in his eyes. "Two years ago today," he said, "I buried my son, Jeff. He died of AIDS."

Herman told me some of his story, some of Jeff's story. "I did not approve of his lifestyle," Herman told me, "but he was my son and I loved him."

When Jeff's lover left him in the wake of his diagnosis, Jeff moved back home with his father. Both Herman and his son were active in a church. They were very devout and regularly attended services. When Jeff was diagnosed with AIDS and it became known in the church, Jeff experienced condemnation. Their church turned its back. Jeff no longer felt welcome at the table of his church.

Herman, however, stayed at the table even though he felt his church had betrayed him and his son. He stayed until the day Jeff died. Herman called his pastor and told him about Jeff's death and invited him to the wake service. When the pastor did not show up to mourn with him the death of his son, Herman said simply, "There was no room for me at the table of that church."

Herman found a place at another table in another church. His conversion is directly linked to the death of his son. You see, when Jeff was dying and Herman could no longer take care of all his needs, Jeff went to a hospice where a woman named Kate served as chaplain. Kate treated Jeff with such compassion that Herman knew his son could die in peace. "He loved Kate," Herman said. When Jeff died, Kate conducted Jeff's funeral.

Because of this woman's fidelity to Jeff; because of her willingness to wash the feet of his son, to hold him in his fear, to serve him in his last days, Herman found a place at the table again.

In these years since Jeff's death, every so often Herman visits the hospice where his son died. Even if Kate isn't there, he just sits for a while and remembers. He remembers the compassion his son found there. He remembers the faith he found there. He remembers this place where his son discovered understanding, where his son's story was reverenced and respected, where his son found the courage to die.

One night, as he was leaving this place that held so many memories, so much hope, he told me how he was still struggling with the sense of betrayal by the church of his childhood, the church he had belonged to for so long. He was in the process of joining Kate's church, the Catholic Church, something a few years before he would never have dreamed of doing. Herman was anguishing over this decision that at first seemed to him so logical and clear. Now, however, as he walked in the cool, crisp air of an autumn evening, he was having doubts. Was he turning his back on the church, on the faith, he had loved so long because they turned their back on him? Was his movement toward the table of another faith motivated only because of his sense of betrayal?

That night as he walked to his car after visiting the hospice where his son had died, he whispered a prayer to his son, Jeff. Am I making the right decision? Are my intentions pure and holy, and not the result of the anger I am still holding?" Herman could not articulate what happened next. He could not put words to the experience. As he stood at his car and looked up at the sky crowded with stars, he felt a wave of awe, of peace, overwhelm him. "All I can say," Herman told me, "and it may sound strange, is that I felt this sense of Jeff's passing over me. I felt comforted. I felt that I was making this decision not out of anger or resentment at the way my son was treated by my church but because of the compassion and peace he found at the table of a woman named Kate who cared for him."

We Know Such a Place

We know such a place, don't we? We've sat at such a table before. We've known the joy of being at the table in the company of friends. When we allow those memories to pass over us, we experience redemption.

As they pass over us, like empty vessels on the table we allow these memories to fill us with hope. For as our ancestors of old celebrated the Passover as a perpetual institution, a night to remember their liberation, so we remember all those people with whom we have gathered through the years who have liberated our love, freed our fears, shared the food of their table and the drink of their dreams. We remember those who have welcomed us to their table and washed our feet with the favor of their friendship. At this rest stop, we drink deeply of these memories and listen for the reason why these people and their actions mean so much. We listen for that holy invitation: "As I have done, so you must do."

We also know those places where we've experienced the pain of rejection, the brutal reality of betrayal. We must not forget those places, those tables, those people at this rest stop. For it was "on the night he was betrayed" that Jesus came to the table in the company of his friends and in the most intimate gesture of love said to them, said even to those who would betray and deny him, "This is my body. This is my blood."

With sacred gestures and simple words, Jesus invested the ritual of Passover with a new meaning, a new memory. Now he became the Passover lamb, the one who would pass over from life to death to life again. "Whenever you do this, remember me."

Whenever we do this — stay at the table even with those who would betray our friendship, deny our relationship, insult our integrity or seek to damage our dignity — we live the memory.

Whenever we do this — gather in the company of friends to tell the stories of God's real presence, God's real passion, God's real promise — we live the memory.

Whenever we do this — find room at the table for those who have been pushed away — we live the memory.

Whenever we do this — wash the feet those whose feet have grown cold, whose hopes have grown old, whose dreams have died too soon — we live the memory.

Whenever we do this — invest the bread with our very selves and say, "This is my body, which will be given up for you" — we live the memory.

Whenever we do this — invest the cup of wine with our compassion and our fidelity and say, "This is my blood, the blood of the new covenant" — we live the memory.

As a community of priestly people of faith at this rest stop of the soul, we commit ourselves to "do this" — to make this table open to all, to reverence and respect each one's story, to hold in the chalice of our hearts each one's pain, to get down on our knees and wash each one's feet. And when we do — when we love one another with that burning desire that leads from this table to the garden and then to the cross — in our emptiness we will hear God whisper:

"I know a place, I'll meet you there."

THE PLACE OF THE SKULL

Though the odor of betrayal persists in the air at the rest stop of the table, it is still a comfortable space where stories of memory and hope are told. Though we are aware of some of the tensions around the table, tensions caused by predictions of betrayal and denial that threatened to tear us apart, we want to stay at the table. We don't want this meal of memory to end. We want to stay at this table in the company of these friends because even with the tensions there is a sense that life doesn't get any better than this: finding a place at a table with those we love, telling stories, toasting friendship, sipping wine, breaking bread.

We must move on, however. Our host does not allow us to stay the night at the table rest top. Before the night is over we make our way to a garden where the wine takes its toll and sleep becomes a friend.

When we finally awake, we find ourselves at another place, the most uncomfortable of places. In the fog of our awakening, we hear God say, "I know a place outside the city gates."

This is our next rest stop. John's passion story describes this rest stop:

> So they took Jesus, and he went out, bearing his own cross, to the site called the Place of the Skull, which in Hebrew is called Golgotha. There they crucified him, and with him two others, one on either side, with Jesus between them (John 19: 17-18).

How odd that last phrase sounds: "with Jesus between them." Jesus is in the middle. Though we know he was always in the middle of conflict and controversy, though we know he was always in the thick of peoples' lives, he found himself in the middle not because he was moderate but because he was always walking on the edge. He was always moving the center of religious belief and social custom out to the fringe. He was always challenging religious institutions and social structures to be more open, more inclusive. Because of this, he was often caught "between them."

Now he is crucified between two convicted criminals. This is the ultimate exclusion, the place of execution: death on a cross at a place outside the holy city.

During his life, this is where we often found him: at a place on the edge, on the fringe, with those people who had been pushed away from the table. Jesus always stayed off the median; he was always on the side of the road, on the shoulder. Because of the place where he lived, he would also die on the edge of the city, outside the gates. Finally, he found himself in between — in the middle of the condemned.

Because he identified himself with those who were most often excluded, this is where we find him at this crucial moment: at a place of the skull, the place of the condemned, the place of execution.

And God says to us, "I'll meet you here. At this place. At this cross."

We've all been to this place before, haven't we? Some of us more than others. Some of us have been here many times. There is nothing comfortable about this place. Indeed, this is the most difficult, the most dangerous, the most destructive place in which we ever find ourselves. Yet we've all been here, haven't we?

I remember being in this place many years ago in the first parish where I served. I remember the woman's name: Donna. I never met her, but I met her husband once, briefly. Our visit had been long enough for him to call me the day Donna died.

"My wife is dead," he said. "Donna is dead." It happened in a car accident on the way home from Des Moines. This was her husband's request: "Will you help me tell my two boys that their mom won't be coming home?" The boys were three and six.

Ironically, earlier that day I had been the answer man for high school seniors who were studying issues of death and dying. I had told them, "I have no answers." It was honest and true. However, I told them I also had hope. Yet when Donna's husband called, I wasn't so sure. How does one tell a three-year-old that his mom won't be coming home?

To sustain others in a moment of sorrow is about all one can do. That simply reminds them of something: "You are not alone." But a three-year-old? Death has no dominion here. Only a mother's love has meaning. How does one say, "Your mom who has held you, fed you, healed you, kissed you and wiped your tears won't be coming home?"

I never met Donna. But I met her sons. I held them in my arms. It was all I knew to do.

We've all been to such a place. When we're in this place, our bodies reflect what we are feeling. We carry the weight of the world on our shoulders. When we are called or freely choose to help another carry the pain of his or her loss, knowledge of our own loss empties us and makes room for the other. But our bodies are weighed down.

When we are in such a place as this, this weight pushing down on our bodies takes its toll. For some, the mind breaks down. For most, the heart breaks. For all of us who have ever stood in such a place of death, the soul begins to crack under the pressure, under the weight of another's loss. When the soul cracks, an energy is released. It's an energy not our own. It's an energy we know as God.

It is this energy of God that draws us to this rest stop even when we don't know why. We can't explain it. Our mind tells us to stay away. This place of death is not safe. No, it is not a safe place. However, the energy released within us when our soul cracks open with our own pain and the pain of others sends adrenaline, if not answers, and says, "This is not a safe place but rather a place to be saved."

MEETING AT THE CROSS

At this rest stop of the cross where we meet, we are amazed by his appearance: "So marred is his look beyond that of humans" (Isaiah 52: 14). His appearance is so shocking that nations are startled and kings stand speechless.

Who would believe we could meet at such a place? Who would believe that this one with "no stately bearing to make us look at him, no appearance that would attract us to him, a man avoided and spurned by others, a man of suffering, accustomed to infirmity, one of those from who people hide their faces, one who is held in no esteem" (Isaiah 52: 2-3), who would believe that through this one the will of God is to be accomplished? Yet this place of the skull, Golgotha, this unsafest of rest stops, is the very place where we are saved.

The longer we stay at this rest stop, the longer we look, the soul energy that has been released from our own crushing experiences begins to stir and flow within our bodies. Could it be that it was our infirmities he bore, our sufferings he endured? We thought when we arrived at this place and saw his marred appearance, the shocking sight of his bruised and bloody body that this one in the middle, this one who spent his life on the edge, was being punished for some unmentionable crime. After all, he is in a place where the worst criminals are taken to die. This is the place of execution. This is not the place where dreams or dreamers go to die. This is the place of retribution, not repentance; a place of revenge, not reconciliation.

The longer we stay, however, the longer we look, the energy within us grows. Questions rise to the surface: Could it be that he was pierced for our offenses? Could it be that he was crushed for our sins?

We stand in place. We don't walk away. We don't move, and yet something moves within us. We sense that this one, so broken, so bloody, so bruised, is somehow healing us. In a place where retribution was the order of the day, repentance begins to replace revenge. Pardon replaces punishment. The feeling inside grows ever more: By his wounds we are healed.

How can this be? We trace our wounds. How we have wandered far, trying to make it on our own, astray, betrayer and betrayed, following our own way. Yet we are not punished for walking the other way. We are not reprimanded. Instead, this one who hangs in the balance between heaven and earth carried in his body our guilt, our shame.

We remember that at the table he said, "This is my body, which will be given up for you" (Luke 22: 19). We look now at this body, naked but without shame. "This is my body."

He remains silent. Though harshly treated, he opens not his mouth. Oppressed and condemned, he dies. It's over. The end. He said it himself just before he died, "It is finished" (John 19: 30). Still we stand there, unable to dismiss this feeling, this energy, growing inside. It's a feeling that there must be something more, something we're missing. Is this his destiny? Is this our destiny? To be taken down from this cross, cut off forever from the land of the living? Is this all there is?

His lifeless body is taken down from the cross. And now, as the feeling grows ever stronger that this one who spoke truth, who had done no wrong, who healed the sick and raised the dead, has not deserved this destiny, a whisper from deep within rises: "I know another place. I'll meet you there."

We don't know what this means or where this place might be. It couldn't be the unmarked grave where they place this one's body, could it? It couldn't be the tomb where this one is laid to rest. This is not our next meeting place, is it? Of course not. It doesn't make any sense.

It's time to go. The cross is now empty. The body is gone. We take one last look at the empty cross and begin to walk away. We try to make sense of this scene, this gruesome spectacle. No words come to mind. There is nothing to say. How do you tell a three-year-old boy his mother will not be coming home? Arms outstretched, there is nothing left to do but to hold on for dear life. "Woman, there is your son. There is your mother" (John 19: 26-27).

Holding on to one another, we stop and look once more at the empty cross. They say the tomb is close at hand. The whisper returns: "I know another place. I'll meet you there."

Holding on for dear life, we leave the empty cross, knowing that the tomb will be full — at least for a few days. As we walk on, the whisper calls back to us: "I know the place. I'll meet you here again in three days."

Right Place, Right Time

At the end of our seven-day sojourn, we find ourselves in the right place at the right time. The rest stops of Holy Week capture the whole of life. We are like a certain group of disciples who went to their master and asked what places he had passed through in his journey. Thereupon the master said:

"God first led me by the hand into the place of action, and there I dwelt for several years. Then God returned and led me to the place of sorrow, where I lived until my heart was purged of every attachment. Then I found myself in the place of love, where burning flames consumed whatever was left in me of self. This brought me to the place of silence, where the mysteries of life and death were bared before my wondering eyes."

"Was this the final place of your quest?" the disciples asked.

"No," the master said. "One day God said, 'Today I shall take you to the innermost sanctuary of the temple, to the very heart of God.' And I was led to the place of joy."

This is redemption's eternal rest stop: a place of joy. Like Mary, we rise early in the morning on the first day of the week, while it is still dark. The whisper within us has grown ever stronger: "I know another place. I'll meet you there." This whisper becomes a shout on the seventh day: "Wake up, sleepy heart! Go to the tomb! I'll meet you there."

Like Mary, we roll out of bed and make our way to the tomb. What we see there is beyond belief. The stone has been moved away! Mary doesn't understand this either. She starts running away — in the opposite direction. Back to her friends, who are still huddled in grief and in fear. She has astonishing news: "The stone has been rolled away! Wake up! The tomb is empty! Hurry! I'll meet you there."

Peter and John race to redemption's final rest stop — the tomb. The younger one, who has the legs of a sprinter and the heart of a long-distance runner, arrives at the tomb first. He does not enter this meeting place but instead bends low and looks inside. A few moments later, the older one, out of shape and out of breath from the events of the past few days, comes to the rest stop, panting, praying. Even in his breathless state, this one is bold as ever. He storms into the tomb, this meeting place, this empty room, and sees the wrappings on the ground. He doesn't know what to think, what to say. His friend comes into the empty tomb. He looks around and believes.

The events of these last seven days, all the places we've been, all the rest stops where we've stayed, come back to mind and heart and lead us to this place of joy. We remember the invitation to empty ourselves, to become as empty as possible, so that the new life that God offers us at this place of our destiny can fill us to the brim.

We have spent the last seven days of this trip emptying the vessels of our lives of self-interest and selfish concerns. In this process of emptying, we have found ourselves at a table in the company of friends, at a cross, holding on to one another for dear life, and now at a tomb, empty of death and filled with life.

The emotional roller coaster that brought us to this place of joy where the stone on the tomb has been rolled away has taken us on the ride of a lifetime. It gives us a new lease on life, a new appreciation of life. The rest stops on this journey of the soul reminds us not to take life for granted, not to take each other for granted.

When we are surprised by life in a place where we expected only death, the experience takes hold of us and won't let go. It takes us to new places, places we've never been to before, to tell the story of life's victory over death.

Peter, after searching the empty tomb and finding no sign of death, never forgets this experience. He continues to tell this redemption story again and again (cf. Acts 10: 34-43). He tells the story by reminding his listeners of all the places associated with the life, death and resurrection of Jesus. He traces those places in Jesus' life — beginning in Galilee, through Judea "where he went about doing good works and healing all who were in the grip of the devil" (v. 38). He speaks of Jerusalem where he was "put to death by hanging him on a tree" (v. 39). He identifies the Risen One in terms of a another place, Jesus of *Nazareth*, as he talks about that third day when he and John ran breathlessly to the tomb, only to find the stone had been rolled away and the tomb empty.

Then Peter tells the most remarkable part of this resurrection story. He talks about all those places where the Risen One appeared, "not to all the people, but to us who were chosen by God as witnesses, and who ate and drank with him after he rose from the dead" (v. 41).

LISTEN FOR THE SOUND OF OUR NAME

The first of these appearances occurs on that seventh day, the first day of the week, after John and Peter have gone home. Mary stays for a while at the rest stop, "weeping outside the tomb." While she is conversing with the angels, she turns around and sees Jesus standing there. She thinks he is the gardener. She is convinced someone has stolen the body and moved her beloved to another place. "Sir, if you have carried him away, tell me where you have laid him, and I will take him away" (John 20: 1-9).

It is only when Jesus calls Mary by name that she recognizes him. We can imagine Jesus saying to Mary, "I told you about this place. I told you I'd meet you here." Mary, filled with joy, clings to Jesus. Yet this empty tomb rest stop says we cannot cling to the Risen One. Now that we have arrived at this new place in the world, we must continue the journey by telling others what we have seen and heard.

At last we have arrived at this place called joy. After God has taken us by the hand and led us through places of action and sorrow, places of love and places of silence, we have finally arrived at this place of joy. God knows this place. God has told us this is the place where we would meet. But now we must move on. Now we must leave this place. We are willing to do so only because we know deep in our souls that this place will never leave us.

The joy we experience at this rest stop of the soul reminds us that the empty tomb is not a hiding place. It is a revealing place, a place without boundaries or limits. The roller coaster ride of our lives stops here at this place, but our joyride is just beginning. Indeed, we take this place with us wherever we go as we make a conscious decision each and every day to live joyfully on the journey.

When we know the place of joy in our lives, we are in the right place at the right time.

REST STOP

HOMECOMING:
WELCOME
TO THE HEARTLAND

We have to stumble through so much dirt and humbug before we reach home. And we have no one to guide us. Our only guide is our homesickness.

— Herman Hesse, *Steppenwolf*

Taking a Ride on a Carousel

Chapter Ten

For every soul is a circus.
And every mind is a tent,
And every heart is a sawdust ring
Where the circling race is spent.

                 – Vachel Lindsay

Come, come, whoever you are,
Wanderer, worshipper, lover of leaving — it doesn't matter,
Ours is not a caravan of despair.
Come, even if you have broken your vow a hundred times.
Come, come again, come.

                 – Jelaluddin Rumi

On this trail of transformation, we have explored the nature of creation, incarnation and redemption stories and reflected on how they shape the soul and spark conversion. In these final chapters as we turn toward home, we will visit a few rest stops in a land where each of us has a residence: the heartland.

A few years ago, the first sign a traveler would see upon entering the state of Iowa (the home of Story City) was "Welcome to the Heartland." Since Iowa is geographically in the center of the United States, the slogan seemed appropriate. Even more than a welcome sign, however, it can be seen as an invitation to sojourners to spend some time in this not-so-strange land of the heart.

On our journey so far, we have discovered that being a pilgrim is a state of heart. As our redemption stories have reminded us, when our hearts are broken open, the boundaries of this state become less visible. Still, we know when we have crossed the state line. We know the signs: Buckle Up for Safety, It's the Law; Speed Limits Strictly Enforced; Road Workers Ahead, Give Them a Brake.

This is the land where dreams are planted and memories make the soil rich and fertile. This is a place where suffering is sown and tears are welcome because they water the land. It is a land where skyscrapers scuff the bottom side of heaven and hot air balloons, looking like colorful exclamation points as they return to earth, provide perfect punctuation.

No state sticker is required to reside in the heartland since the authorities will know you live here, you belong here, because of the creases on your face and the smile in your eyes. Joy lines are the only kind allowed on this map of the heartland. These authorities, the people who patrol this land where borders are invisible and boundaries ever changing, have lived here a long time. They are authorities precisely because they lived here long ago when the heartland was small — so tiny, in fact, that the "welcome to" and "come again" signs were back-to-back. They know that one cannot live in the heartland that has no boundaries unless one has first known the borders of one's life. How small they can become at times. After a while, one sees these borders stretch because the land is too small to hold all the people who want to move in. Friends and family members and even a foe or two move into the neighborhood, and the city limits have to expand. The decision to extend the limits is not held behind closed doors in the councils of the mighty but on the street in conversations with the weak.

Soon one discovers that there is always room for one more resident. "Do you mind if I have a look around?" a visitor asks. A few stories are told. Since, as Anthony de Mello said, "The shortest distance between a human being and Truth is a story," this new friend says, "I'd like to purchase a plot in your heartland."

You, in turn, say, "Welcome home," because in the long run you realize it is a short walk from here to love.

Even if you move, this new friend stays. That's the magic of having another person reside in your heartland. Soon your heartland is crowded but not overpopulated. The increase of people means more services are required. Taxes must be raised, not in terms of currency but in terms of time. Though the ones who live here in your heartland may live far away, they are always near. That is because when one lives in the heartland, distance is not defined by geography but by memory. You do not forget the names on the mailboxes that crowd your heartland. These are the people who over the years have moved in and made their home here. One lives on letters and long-distance phone calls late at night. "Keep in touch" is not a throwaway line but a promise of proximity and real presence.

On this last leg of our journey of transformation we yearn to return to this heartland. Here we recall the people who have caused our souls to stretch and to believe that no matter how far one travels or how often one leaves, there is no place like home.

And no experience like coming home to the heartland.

So, buckle up for safety, slow down, and give yourself a break. Remember, in the heartland speed limits are strictly enforced.

THE CIRCUS OF THE SOUL

Our first rest stop in the heartland is to visit Story City, Iowa, again. One of Story City's main attractions is a restored 1913 Hershel-Spillman merry-go-round. This carousel — which features not only wooden horses but also pigs, chickens and dogs, a chariot, a "whirling" tub, two benches, gargoyles, a canvas mural and a 1936 Wurlitzer organ — was placed on the National Register of Historic Places in 1986. According to the Story City Chamber of Commerce, which purchased the carousel in 1938, it is one of only 248 existing all-wood, hand-carved carousels left in the United States.

Story City's antique carousel serves as a symbol of the time when our lives were less hectic, when the pace of life seemed slower. It's a reminder of Sundays in the park with the family or picnics on a summer afternoon. The fact that so few of these carousels still exist may cause us to lament their passing. It may cause us to ponder the reasons why they have been replaced by more exciting rides at amusement parks that promise breathtaking speed and deliver thrills that send chills through one's body and soul. The rapid heartbeat one experiences on modern-day roller coasters is more reflective of today's race than the measured pace of the old-time merry-go-round. The carousel seems out of date. Speed has replaced stride. The lessons from our youth that taught us to "walk, don't run" have been reversed.

Or have they? One of the ancient cries of youth, "I'm running off to join the circus!" captures this spirit of keeping on the move. Even though the circus may have a carousel to show us how to slow down as we go round and round, other images of the circus we call the soul keep us on the go.

When we are busy and stressed out, someone may ask us, "How's life?" And we may respond, "My life is a three-ring circus!" The poet, Vachel Lindsay, understood this concept when in 1928 he wrote:

> For every soul is a circus.
> And every mind is a tent,
> And every heart is a sawdust ring
> Where the circling race is spent.

In the hectic pace of life when we feel spent by the "circling race," we seek some balance at the rest stop of the circus. In the world of the imagination, the *nation* of *images*, then, our first stop is under the big top.

As we examine this image of the soul as a circus, it may be helpful to connect with a bit of history. John Bill Ricketts presented the first circus ever seen in America on April 3, 1792. The big tent went up at 12th and Market streets in Philadelphia. Actually, there was no big tent because this circus was mainly an equestrian show with a few tumblers, jugglers and clowns for comic relief. It was a very intimate kind of theater with folks gathered in a circle around the performers.

The man most identified with the circus, P.T. Barnum, was in semi-retirement when he realized the potential entertainment value of the circus. So in the late 1870s, the master entrepreneur, together with James A. Bailey, produced "The Greatest Show on Earth." Barnum and Bailey are credited (or discredited) with turning the intimacy of the circus into a spectacle with three, and sometimes as many as seven, rings of performers at a time. Though there are some fifty smaller circuses traveling the country and setting up their tents today, a major circus like Ringling Brothers now has a "big top" made of concrete instead of canvas, as it sets up in large arenas in major cities.

Many of us hold special memories of attending the circus when we were children. I recall a conversation during supper one evening that was sparked by a report on the evening news about the annual circus wagon parade outside of Milwaukee. The people at the table shared stories about the time the circus came to their small towns in middle America. Those who were speaking were savoring memories of the joy they found when the circus came to town. As Ernest Hemingway once wrote, the circus "is the only spectacle I know that while you watch it gives the quality of a truly happy dream."

Beyond our treasured childhood memories of going to the circus, there are also certain phrases that now seem standard in English usage which had their origin in the circus. These phrases find new meaning in the soul's vocabulary. For example, "rain or shine" was the saying used on circus advertising to assure people "the show will go on" regardless of the weather since the circus played under a tent. "Hold your horses" was a call to tell those riding horses in the circus parade to hold up when the elephants were on the way. This was important since horses tend to panic at the sight and smell of elephants. "Let's get the show on the road" was the circus call when the show was ready to move on from one town to the next.

These three phrases help uncover some truths in the language of soul. When push comes to shove, most people genuinely believe in the future. We will continue "rain or shine." Even though some are saying, "hold your horses," in panic at the elephant-like changes that charge and threaten to stampede the status quo, there are those prophetic pilgrims among us who are ever saying, "let's get the show on the road," to capture the missionary zeal of our uncommon corporate enterprise as soul explorers.

Another phrase that found its birth in circus lingo is "Get on the bandwagon!" Legend has it that a famous circus entrepreneur was riding on the bandwagon that was leading his parade through town. When he spotted his friend Zachary Taylor in the crowd, he yelled, "Come up here where people can see who's going to be their next president! Get on the bandwagon!"

After our experience at the empty tomb, this becomes a most fitting invitation for those of us still standing in the shadows of the crowd and waving as the parade of life passes us by.

When Life is a Three-Ring Circus

As life pulls us up on the bandwagon and draws us on the journey of transformation through the heartland, we sometimes find ourselves in a rush to get to where we're going. We've been on the road a long time. We want to get home.

In our haste, the bandwagon seems to pick up speed. The carousel that reminded us of a simpler, slower time now is thrust into high gear, and the merry-go-round accelerates. Our life spins out of control as we scream, "Stop this merry-go-round, I want to get off!" Even when the carousel stops, however, and we climb down, dizzy, trying to regain our balance, someone throws us balls or bowling pins or even flaming torches and says, "Here, juggle these!" Suddenly, we find our lives have become like a three-ring circus as we try to juggle all our responsibilities on our homeward trek through the heartland.

When our lives become like a three-ring circus, it is necessary to stop, get off the merry-go-round, drop the responsibilities, if just for a while, and look closely at those three rings that compose our lives: our goals and purpose, our family and relationships, and our work. In the language of the soul, the three rings that attract our attention are called spirituality, community and ministry. For most of us, the trick is how to balance these areas because they often seem to be at war with one another. But remember: All three rings are under "the big top." Though the spotlight shifts from one to another, there is activity going on in all three rings all the time. It's only when the spotlight stays on only one ring for a long time that the other two areas of our lives are left in the dark. And that is when we find ourselves out of balance.

I would define the center ring, **spirituality**, as the "stuff" of our life — the core, the heart and soul of who we are. Too often we think about our spiritual life as somehow separate from our social life or our personal life or our family life or our work life. We compartmentalize our lives too much. This may result in allowing us to be very organized, but it also reflects an understanding of spirituality as a slot to be filled rather than a soul that flourishes in all we are and all we do. There is not a spiritual side of things so much as a spiritual center for all things. We nurture that spiritual center through prayer, worship, solitude, sacraments and conversations with God and with close friends.

In this center ring of spirituality there is a hook suspended from the ceiling. From this hook our lives hang in the balance. It is noteworthy that in the language of the soul a hook looks like a question mark since the spiritual life always poses more questions than it provides answers.

For most of us, the second ring of **community** reflects our family, but also includes friends and those significant others we rely on in life to inspire us, challenge us, wonder and weep with us.

The third ring is reserved for our **ministry** or the "work" that we do. Remember that in the soul's vocabulary "ministry" is all the work that comprises our lives. It is not only church-related activities but also our livelihoods that put bread on the table, clothes on our children and a roof over our heads. All our work is, or can be, an adventure in furthering the reign of God.

Taken together under the big tent we call our lives, these three rings of spirituality, community and ministry raise three important questions. Our spirituality asks, "Who am I?" Our relationships in community ask, "To whom do I belong?" And our ministry raises the issue of "What should I do — not only for a living but for a life?"

Our lives spell out the answers to these questions as we seek to find a healthy spirituality that balances our ministry (the work we do) and our community (who we are in relationship to others). For example, one of the complaints I often hear from people who come for spiritual companionship is that they don't find enough time to pray because of all the commitments they have to keep. Their valid concern reminds me of the story about the cobbler who went to the rabbi and said, "Tell me what to do about my morning prayer. My customers are poor people who have only one pair of shoes. I pick up their shoes late in the evening and work on them most of the night; at dawn there is still work to be done if the people are to have their shoes ready before they go to work. Now my question is: What should I do about my morning prayer?"

"What have you been doing?" the rabbi asked.

"Sometimes I rush through the prayer quickly and get back to my work, but I then feel bad about not spending enough time with God. At other times I let the hour of prayer go by. Then too I feel a sense of loss and every now and then, as I raise my hammer from the shoes, I can almost hear my heart sigh: What an unlucky man I am, that I am not able to make morning prayer."

The rabbi responded, "If I were God, I would value the sigh more than the prayer."

In the three-ring circus that sometimes characterizes our lives, it is important to steal away a few quiet moments each day and spend time in prayer. But when the day has almost slipped away and time and energy have been spent, remember a sigh that echoes from the heart will bend God's ear. And since God is the ultimate ringmaster of this circus, we will come to know that "the show must go on."

PAY ATTENTION: THE BUSYNESS OF LIFE

There is a certain rhythm to life — a delicate balance between work and relationships, community and solitude — that must be maintained to sustain creative energy. In a task-oriented world, where the focus is often on the work that must be accomplished, it is easy to neglect adequate time for leisure and to overlook the need for nurturing personal relationships. We even lose touch with those who are most important in our lives.

The late Paul Tsongas, who ran for president in 1992, offered an important insight into this need for balance and rhythm in life. In an interview a few years before he ran for president, Tsongas was explaining why in the early 1980s he resigned from the United States Senate when he was diagnosed with cancer. He told the reporter: "I never heard of anyone on his death bed saying, I wish I had spent more time at the office." He gave up his Senate seat to spend time with his family. His cancer went into remission, he regained his strength, and in the early 1990s he was healthy enough to make a run for the presidency.

On November 2, 1992, the day before the election, Paul Tsongas learned that his cancer had returned. In another interview, he said: "When I learned I had cancer again, I was frightened, but cancer is no longer a mystery. I've absorbed it emotionally. My view is that you grow by adversity. It's the dread of being removed from the scene that makes you appreciate being on the scene. If you presume endless days, then no day has particular value. I think of all the fathers who have young children and play golf all day Saturday and Sunday. They've never had cancer. I think of the husbands who never voice their affection for their wives. They've never had cancer . . . . These past ten years have been much richer because I appreciate my wife and my children."

Ultimately, a spirituality of balance begins with recognizing the value and importance of relationships: our relationships with God, with those we love the most and with ourselves. This is soulful stuff.

So notice, please, that at the entrance to the big tent in this circus of the soul, there is a sign: "Pay Attention." This is the only cost for attending the circus of the soul; this is the entrance fee that will admit us to the greatest show on earth. We "pay" with our "attention."

That may seem like a small price to pay. However, the serious ailment that plagues some children, "attention deficit disorder," seems to afflict many of us adults. We no longer "pay attention" to each other. This makes the price of admission to the circus very steep indeed because we are operating out of a deficit. And the biggest "deficit" of not paying attention as we grow into adulthood is discovered when we inventory our dreams.

When I think back to my youth, there was never a deficit of dreams. Some of these dreams were played out with my younger brother Bob. We would often play baseball in our backyard. We knew how to dream back then. We pretended that the backyard was Busch Stadium and that one of us was the Cardinals while the other was the Giants or Dodgers. We played as if we were fighting for the pennant. Then, after playing out our dreams in the afternoon, we sat on the porch in the evening and listened to the real thing on the radio. Even better, Dad might come home from work and say, "Let's go to the ballgame tonight." We'd sit in the bleachers. Dreams would come true. At least for one night.

Those were the nights I loved my dad the most. I never thought about it much then, but Dad worked close to downtown and we lived out by the airport. So Dad would have to drive all the way back home, grab a quick dinner and then drive all the way back downtown — past where he worked — to Busch Stadium. Once I remember the ballgame was sold out. After standing in line for bleacher tickets for an hour or so, we were turned away. A dream dashed that night. On some nights we would stop at White Castle for a sack of hamburgers and a coke on the way home after the game. Although my stomach no longer can handle a hamburger late in the evening, these times were important to nourish my youthful soul.

I mowed grass during those summers of my youth. It seemed like mindless activity — this was long before I learned how important it is to engage each task, no matter how tedious or uncomplicated, with a spirit of mindfulness. Now I understand how soulful it was to mow the grass. My mind would wander aimlessly as I pushed the mower, but soul was engaged. And when soul is engaged, daydreams are born.

Simple tasks like washing the dishes or mowing the lawn become soulful activities. Our intellect slows down while our imagination is engaged. The simplicity of the activity frees the sacred imagination to dream.

In our search for balance, some common, ordinary household utensils might help us find our soul again. For example, a few years ago my spiritual director gave me a wooden spoon that I keep on my prayer table at home. It is a prayerful reminder to always "stir the soup" and taste it myself before I serve it to others. At the spiritual center of our lives, we stir our soul with images of God and our own experiences. When we taste this soup in our silent prayer, we know immediately whether it needs more of that Gospel ingredient "salt of the earth." Without this essential element, we will never be able to flavor our work or sprinkle our relationships with the zesty taste of God. In the silence of prayer, we savor the flavor of our faith and only then seek to serve.

For people with a bent toward busyness, however, quiet moments of prayer in the circus rest stop of the soul are rare unless they are scheduled in. I recall the story of a priest who was called by a member of his parish. She wanted to see him the next day at 2:30 PM. "I'm sorry," the priest said, "I have another appointment at that time." Understanding how busy the priest was, the parishioner said she would see him later in the week.

Well, the next day, at precisely 2:30, the parishioner was driving through the city park. Suddenly she saw the priest sitting under a tree, reading a book. She couldn't believe it. She stopped the car and rushed over to him, her face flushed with anger. Before she could speak, however, the priest held up his hand and said, "Please, can't you see I have another appointment."

Spending time with a good book, writing in a journal, sitting under a tree on a warm summer day, these activities and others like them increase our attention span. They do more for our soul than we dare to imagine or care to admit.

CONFRONTING OUR FEARS

After paying attention and gaining entrance to the big top, we soon discover that the circus of the soul engages two of our basic human emotions: fear and joy. We are gripped by fear as we watch the lion trainer take the wild beasts through their paces or gaze in awe toward the top of the big tent as high-wire aerialists walk a tightrope hundreds of feet above our heads. And we find some joy as we laugh at the ludicrous antics of the clowns.

The big top is a good place to observe both of these emotions. Let's first take a good look at our fear. If fear is a constant companion, if we find ourselves being afraid of change, being afraid of the dark areas of our lives, being afraid of death, we might learn something from the circus. Imagine that aerialist who walks without a net, balancing himself on a thin wire. As he walks the wire, we see how his wire is a thin line between life and death. One slip, one misstep, one move not in balance, and he falls to his death. He must be focused, and he must be passionate about his work. If he is careless or indifferent about a particular performance, it might be his last.

The high-wire artist must have some fear when he stands on the platform. If the fear were overwhelming, he would not be able to take the first step. A healthy fear, however, can be controlled. Moreover, the energies of this emotion we call fear can be harnessed to effect an even greater performance in walking the taut tightrope of tensions inherent in living under the big top.

Several years ago there was a well-known television circus show that developed a tiger act. Like the rest of the show, it was done "live" before a large audience. One evening, the tiger trainer went into the cage with several tigers to do a routine performance. The door was locked behind him. The spotlights highlighted the cage, the television cameras moved in close and the audience watched in suspense as the trainer skillfully put the tigers through their paces.

In the middle of the performance, however, a power failure caused the lights to go out. As technicians hurriedly tried to start the backup generator, the trainer stood in the dark of a locked cage with the tigers. To say the very least, this placed the trainer at a tremendous disadvantage since tigers are able to see in the dark and it takes some time for human eyes to adjust. So there the trainer was standing in the dangerous darkness, seemingly defenseless, armed with only a whip and a small kitchen chair. Yet when the lights came on thirty seconds or so after they had gone out, the trainer calmly finished his performance without incident.

Afterwards, reporters asked him how he felt when the lights went out. He admitted that he was scared to death because he realized the tigers could see him but he could not see them. The trainer told the reporters that he confronted this fear by remembering that the tigers did not know that he could not see them. So he kept cracking his whip as he had done before when the lights were on. Nothing changed in his performance even though the lights were off. His approach to the tigers was the same whether the lights were on or not.

Since we've all faced tigers in the dark now and then, the tiger trainer's experience and how he approached his fear might offer us some insight when we experience a power failure and the lights go out under our big top. The Scripture story that surfaces in the soul in such situations is the one about the night the disciples were lost in the storm at sea. Like the trainer trapped with the tigers in the dark, they were terrified. We know the feeling when forces of evil in the world beyond our control turn out the lights in our lives. We know the fear when incidents of sin in our own souls scare us half to death. We know the feeling when insecurities rise from within us as we seek to live out our call and find some balance in the three rings of our lives. We know the feeling when the ghosts of past experiences hiding in the closets of our souls come out to haunt us every now and then.

How do we respond in such situations? Do we, like the trainer, remain calm and centered, even as our fear threatens to push us out of balance? Or do we respond like the disciples in that Gospel story: "In their fear they began to cry out" (Matthew 14: 26).

Either response, I suppose, is reasonable. Which one, however, reflects the attitude of balance that the soul is always seeking? The tiger trainer approached his perilous situation in the same way he approached the routine of his life. Though his stomach was knotted in fear, his soul was free to remind him that even though he could not see the tigers, they did not know he couldn't see them. So he continued his work as if the lights were on, and he survived.

The disciples, on the other hand, were not so centered. Indeed, the first words of Jesus when he comes to them walking on the water are: "Get a hold of yourselves! It is I! Do not be afraid" (v. 27).

In remembering this story and its connections with our soul's ongoing conversion, we should not forget how this incident of the storm at sea began: "When Jesus had sent his disciples away, he went up on the mountain by himself to pray" (v. 23). Jesus calmed the storm with the calm he experienced in a place of prayer. His ministry (his work) flowed from a place of silent communion with God. His concern for his community (his relationships) was inspired by a contemplative stance before God.

In seeking balance in the three-ring circus of our lives, we too must be nurtured by quiet times of prayerful silence and communion with God. Then, when we run into some dark spaces, a few storms or even a few tigers on the prowl, the invitation is always etched on our memory: "Do not be afraid." These words give us the courage to step out of the boat. They remind us that we can walk the tightrope stretched between life and death while always walking toward the presence of Jesus among us. We can depend on the fact that when the winds of fear blow with hurricane force and cause us to sink, there is a hand stretched out to save us. There's a God-among-us who will catch us when we fall.

Like the trainer in the tiger cage, when it is dark and we are most afraid, God has God's eyes fixed on us: not to devour us but to save us.

When Jesus says, "Do not be afraid," he's not saying fear isn't part of our human experience. He isn't suggesting that we should never have fear. Rather, he is challenging us not to become our fear. Too many of us have become our fears, whether it's fear of change, fear of being different, fear of failure, fear of success, fear of standing alone, fear of community, fear of intimacy or fear of truth. The question the soul invites us to explore is: Under the big top of life, are we willing to stand with one another in our fear? Are we willing to huddle close but not become our fear?

Joy: Send in the Clowns

Now we turn to the other basic emotion we experience in the circus rest stop of the soul: joy. A priest in my community, Father Dan Schaefer, who was the religious superior when I was in the seminary, often referred to us affectionately as "clowns." More than a term of endearment, I think he was onto something about our identity as soul-journers. As we seek to find balance in the three-ring circus of our lives, it is important to ask ourselves: Where do we find joy in life? Have we lost that sense of wonder, of excitement and enthusiasm, of joy? By visiting the circus of the soul, we seek to reclaim the joy by sending for the clowns.

Remember the ancient anthem of youth, "I'm going to run away and join the circus"? There is a sense of nomadic adventure in this youthful cry. It captures a certain kind of zeal for being on the move and living on the fringe. Circus people live their lives on the fringe. They move from town and town, set up their show, perform amazing feats that dazzle children and adults alike, and move on. When they leave, there is a part of us, a part of our soul that yearns for such freedom of expression, that whispers, "What a life!"

In addition to recapturing the innocence and excitement of our youth, the circus metaphor challenges the parameters of our own lives. Circus people, with their movement and their daring deeds, challenge our souls to look at how boring and safe our lives have become. I recall the story about the politician who went to see the priest for counsel because he was feeling that his life had become too routine. The priest advised the politician to go outside the next time it rained and lift his face to heaven. "It will bring a revelation to you," the priest said. A few weeks later the politician came to the rectory. He was very upset. "Father, I followed your advice, but no revelation came. All I got was soaking wet. I felt like a fool."

The priest smiled. "Not a bad revelation for the first try."

Here the soul sings an invitation: When our lives become too safe and secure, send for the clowns. Lighten up, loosen that starchy collar and laugh at what we have become: stationary creatures of habit instead of nomadic characters of whimsical holiness.

"Stability" is not a primary word in the dictionary of the soul. Soulful people are "unstable" people who are on the move. Clowns for Christ. Court jesters of our societal, familial and ecclesial institutions. Harlequins ever moving on the path toward holiness. In effect, soulful people seek always to be saints, but not in the traditional sense captured in the statues we see standing on pedestals in churches. No, it is the kind of sanctity aspired to by soulful people who seek to reflect the face of joy gained simply by being faithful fools for God.

John Shea once said that you can always tell a saint because he or she comes in from left field. To amend that slightly, saints are normally walking on their hands, viewing the world from another perspective: upside-down. Then, as they walk in from left field on their hands, they seek to turn the world upside-down. Perhaps this is how we can identify the saints among us: They walk on their hands as they come in from left field. They are very human and know that holiness is God's gift to them and not something they earn. They know their own sorrow, but instead of being stifled by it they use it to comfort and console those of us who, using our feet instead of our hands, still walk upright and who always seem to be stumbling over first base. Then, when we are on the ground after falling, saints can look us in the eye and say, "Now, look at the world from where you are, from down here, from the grass and the dirt and the astroturf, and see where you want to go: home."

Clowns for God view the world from the ground up, from the upside down. They look ridiculous, seem naive and make great fun of the powers that would be king. They are often told to stop "clowning around." But all they are trying to do is follow the one who walked in the world on his hands and his knees, washing the dusty feet of those too proud to believe.

Clown-saints attempt to settle conflicts with companions who walk this trail of transformation by looking at their own feet first. This can be humbling because clown feet are unusually large and out of proportion. Then the saint looks at the feet of the other to see where he or she stands. Such a ground-up, feet-first perspective gives clown-saints a humble and healing attitude, an attitude of uncommon understanding, an attitude that leads to reconciliation.

Most of us have such clown-saints in our lives, and often they are in our own families. So, perhaps a good spiritual exercise on the road of transformation is not to look at statues of saints in church but to look at photographs in the albums at home. Like little-leaguers poring over pictures of major-league heroes, we can look closely at the photos of family members and friends on these "bubblegum" cards in our family albums and see how these people have invited us to look at the world from a different perspective. We can see the people who have loved us even in those times when we haven't loved ourselves and so couldn't love them because we went zero for four, hit into a couple of double plays, never could get home and even made an error or two. We can fill our prayer spaces with shrines of saints like these: leftfielders who feast on forgiveness and always know how to find their way home.

The saint's challenge is always, each day, to become new. This call to become new is a fool's challenge because the old ways are tried and true. It's the way we've always done things. It's tradition. Oh, we might slap on a fresh coat of paint now and then but only because we don't want to face the fact that the house is falling down.

When we send for the clowns, we don't slap a fresh coat of paint on our houses, we slap some greasepaint on our faces and accept the fool's challenge of becoming a saint.

For one on the circus trail of transformation all that matters is being created anew. Dare we believe that new dreams are waiting to be born? Dare we consider there might be new solutions to old problems? Dare we listen with new ears to words we've heard before? Dare we see familiar faces with new eyes?

Ultimately, this is all that matters. These are the only souvenirs from the circus of life worth saving — belief in our own and each other's goodness, belief in our own and each other's ability to love, belief in our own and each other's dangerous desire to rendezvous at that place of love, of light, of truth, of peace — that place where we are one in joy.

The Spirit-of-the-Clown Christ says, "See, I make all things new." Are we foolish enough to believe that this is not a threat, but an invitation to joy?

In three phrases the clown prophet Micah summarized the three aspects we have been reflecting on in this chapter: spirituality, community and ministry. Micah wrote that this is what God requires of those who visit the circus of the soul — only this:

- ♦ To act justly. (Ministry)
- ♦ To love tenderly. (Community)
- ♦ To walk humbly with your God. (Spirituality)

Act justly. Love tenderly. Walk humbly. We are busy people, and there is so much work to do as we walk on down the road toward home. Every now and then, however, we are reminded of what really matters: the people with whom and for whom we live.

Margaret was in her mid-fifties. She was in the hospital for a routine operation. Only two weeks before, the pastor of the parish where I was serving at the time had witnessed her daughter's wedding. When the pastor visited her in the hospital the day before the surgery, she was still smiling over the memories of that day. Margaret was not anxious about the surgery, simply annoyed. It was a minor inconvenience that interrupted all the work she had been about in preparing for the family's move to another state, which was to take place in a few weeks. She wanted to get the surgery out of the way and get on with her life.

The next morning, Margaret died on the operating table.

When I heard the news that Margaret was dead, the merry-go-round of activity came to a sudden stop. I knew the carousel would start again, the juggling of responsibilities would continue and new crises would arise that would force me to walk the high-wire while trying to keep my balance. But now Margaret's death had focused the spotlight on that ring of relationships in the circus of life. Her death reminded me again that the soul invites us to treasure the possibilities that life presents to us each day in the faces of family and friends.

Whatever stock we place in the stories of people who speak of "near death" experiences, of tunnels filled with light, of seeing friends and family members who have died, conversion is a common refrain in these "near death" experiences. Their lives are changed by the experience of "near death." They no longer fear death because they have "seen the light." Under the circus tent of my soul, Margaret's sudden death focused the spotlight again on how often I suffer from "near life" experiences. I take for granted those I love. I take for granted each day that comes as a gift. I take for granted that I can write that letter, call that friend, tell that story, make amends . . . tomorrow. And so I live "near life" but never truly live.

When we join the circus of the soul, we seek to live each day as if it were our last day. We seek to love without reservation. We seek to live without fear. We say what needs to be said. We tell those we love the words they need to hear. On the carousel of life we clown around with death, smile at the face of death, because we are not afraid. We are ready to die because our fear of death has lost its power, lost its grip. We live each day focused on the only work that really matters:

To act justly, with a reverence and respect for the dignity of others.

To love tenderly, with a care and compassion, a hospitality and a hope that extends to those we love, expressed in words and deeds.

To walk humbly with our God, knowing it is God who guides our days and guards our nights in the circus we call the soul.

Ritual Moments

Chapter Eleven

"I learned one thing."
"What?"
"Never go on trips with anyone you do not love."
     – Ernest Hemingway, *A Moveable Feast*

Do this in memory of me.
     – Luke 22: 19

As we pull up the stakes of our circus tent and continue to walk this trail of transformation through the heartland, we carry with us memories of those moments with family and friends that invoke a sense of coming home. These are the memories that reflect the meaning of "home" because they remind us that when we are with these people, we can be ourselves, we don't have to pretend, we don't have to lie. At the rest stops of the soul that capture our most intimate relationships in life, we understand that there is more than a measure of truth in the old beer commercial that proclaimed, "Life doesn't get any better than this." These moments and memories convey that we don't have to live "near life" but rather encourage us to live in the "now." Even in the difficult or seemingly mundane moments, we are aware that this is life — for better or for worse, this is life.

As we have already suggested, one of the dangers of being a pilgrim people is to assume that we will experience life around the bend, or at the next rest stop, or somewhere down the road. A true conversion takes place on the journey when we avoid the pothole that John Lennon wrote about in one of his songs: "Life is what happens to you while you're making other plans." He was suggesting that our lives are so often occupied with trying to get somewhere else. When we are always looking ahead, we may miss the life that is unfolding right before our eyes.

One way to protect ourselves from falling into this pothole is to recall the rituals we celebrate at these rest stops of the soul. Along with our stories, rituals mark the miles of our journey. These ritual moments, in the words of the master mythologist Joseph Campbell, "give form to human life. Not on a superficial level but at the very depth of one's experience." These rituals speak to the heart and so become the official language spoken in the heartland.

For example, every year on Thanksgiving my family gets together with my aunt and uncle's family. We have been doing this since before I was born, which makes the custom over forty years old. My mom always makes the turkey, dressing (one with and one without raisins), mashed and sweet potatoes, green beans, corn and gravy. Dessert is always pumpkin pie and minced meat pie — my uncle's favorite. (I guess it's an acquired taste.)

During the meal we share stories. We catch each other up on the latest news. We laugh often, sometimes loudly, and maybe even move to a silent space of memory now and then when the name of one no longer with us is mentioned.

After the meal, the men go to the family room and watch football. The women clear the table and do the dishes. At least this was the sexist way we did it for many years. Then a few years ago we finally recognized this discrepancy in our ritual. So a few of us men offered to help with the dishes. Much to our chagrin, we were more than supported by my sisters in this change of ritual servitude. I now make it a point — and part of the ritual every year — to ask Mom why she never has invested in a dishwasher!

When the dishes are clean and put away and the men who have steadfastly refused to get their hands wet in dish water wake up from watching football, the pinochle games begin. One game is in the dining room — the winner's table — the other in the kitchen where the losers go to play their way back into the more prestigious ritual space of the dining room. We play six-handed, double-deck, one-bid pinochle. (Dad instituted the one-bid rule about ten years ago to make the games more exciting.)

More stories are told around these tables. Every year my dad complains that he never holds any good cards. The ritual would not be the same if Dad had any luck on Thanksgiving. After four hours or so of cards, we eat again. Then a final game or two of pinochle before the visitors begin their long ride home.

RITUAL REMINDERS

Rituals provide us with a soul language, a language beyond words for expressing the experience of transformation. Every family has its own set of rituals which in large part have shaped its experience, defined its dreams, molded its memories and fashioned its love as a family. Certain ingredients of the ritual may change over time, like having my mom relax after dinner instead of worrying about the dishes. (She still worries, however, because the sons and sons-in-law may not be as careful with the best china, which, by the way, is used only on Thanksgiving. I hasten to note that each year we plead ignorance as to the proper place for these dishes in the cabinets.) For the most part, however, the ritual action remains the same. I cannot imagine, for example, a Thanksgiving without pinochle. If for some reason one of us would suggest playing pitch or rummy or, God forbid, poker, that one would probably be banished from the family. When new arrivals come into the family through marriage, engagement or "No, Mom, we're just friends," he or she is invited to be initiated into the ritual. (Of course, Dad, the high priest, is not the one who does this initiation rite. We would never consider putting a neophyte with the grand master since his patience is usually gone after the first couple of deals. We wouldn't want to be responsible for breaking up a marriage, an engagement or even "just a friendship.")

These rituals give meaning to our family life. They never become routine. In fact, we depend on the routine, and any change without satisfactory explanation is cause for shaking the foundations of our family's faith.

These ritual moments, simple and sacred, strengthen the bonds of our lives together. They evoke meaning beyond words. They reflect the depth and quality of our love. They are the dock in the harbor we call home that remind us what we must never forget: that we are a family and no matter how rough the sailing or how fierce the storm we will remain a family. We depend on these rituals because they remind us how much we depend on each other.

HAND–ME–DOWN MEMORIES

Rituals enable us to see through the eyes of faith. This quality of vision is different from the way the world sees. The world perceives things in terms of appearance — the bigger, the better. The world perceives things in terms of place — the nicer the neighborhood, the more affluent and therefore the happier people are. The world perceives things in terms of external realities — the more money a family has, the less worries they experience.

Of course, we know this vision is terribly blurred. What matters isn't where we live, but who we are. What matters is the quality of our promise to one another, not the quantity of our possessions. This promise captures the values we hold and the vision for our future that we embrace. This promise is rooted in the reality of God's love, which flourishes in our reverence, our respect and our understanding of each other. Rituals help us celebrate this promise and reflect our concern, our commitment, our love for each other.

It is in the soil of our common life that the seeds of unselfishness are sown — seeds which will grow into a generous spirit.

There are simple rituals in family life that illustrate how we learn to be less selfish and more giving. Take, for example, the ritual of hand-me-down clothes. I was the middle child of five, and I wore my brother's clothes when he outgrew them. My younger brother wore mine when the time came. We passed them down the line. This ritual ceased, of course, when my "little" brother grew to six-foot-three, and I started wearing more black!

My younger brother and I shared a room when we were growing up. We used to fight and complain and raise a little hell until Mom or Dad would come in and tell us to knock it off. We also raised a little heaven as we dreamed out what we would be when we grew up. This is not unusual for families. Though we all need our private space, in a family of seven that was hard to find. We just grew to accept the fact that we were all in this together: What's mine is yours; what's yours is mine.

Rituals reflect this sharing of self. Through stories of what happened at school or at work or at play, by going to little league ballgames and stopping at White Castle for hamburgers afterwards, by sharing pride in a son's first place finish or a daughter's academic achievement, by pasting those pictures made in kindergarten on the refrigerator and bringing out the photo album in the dead of winter to remember the joy of our summer vacation — all these experiences and more become the threads of hope woven into the fabric of family life.

These rituals, then, become the hand-me-down memories that are stored in the closet of our souls and that need to be taken out and dusted off now and then because they teach us that we belong to a group of people who love us as we are. In the good times and in the bad, we remember we have each other and we have God. And more often than not, this is enough. If we pass these memories, these rituals, these values, these truths on to the next generation, then we have made a profound difference. This difference will be reflected in the way we and those who follow us will view this world of ours.

RITUALS FOR THE REIGN OF GOD

Rituals provide us with the words and symbols, sights and scents that bring to mind and heart experiences that are difficult to articulate. In religious terms, the rituals we call sacraments reflect the reality that God is with us. They put into action our belief. The problem, however, is that we often separate the experiences of life from the sacramental rituals we celebrate. Remember the definition of a sacrament we learned in catechism: "A sacrament is an outward sign instituted by Christ to give grace." We need to see the roots of these sacramental moments in the soil of our own faith stories, stories that upon reflection are grace-filled moments where "the glory of God is revealed."

When we cultivate such a sacramental vision, we will know what Malcolm Muggeridge meant when he wrote that his conversion to Catholicism late in his life was a "sense of homecoming, of picking up the threads of a lost life . . . of finding a place at the table that had long been vacant." When he became Catholic, he felt at last that he had found the family he had been looking for throughout his life.

How the sacraments ritualize the experience of conversion was brought home to me several years ago in one of the most moving and memorable moments of my fifteen years of priesthood. It was the night Charley Fox was baptized, confirmed and made his first communion.

Charley was seventy-five years old and had been married to Anna for more fifty-four years. Every Sunday for all those years, Charley drove Anna to church. They raised their six children with Anna's faith. For one reason or another, however, Charley was never baptized or interested in joining the church. All his children, grandchildren and great grandchildren were Catholic, but Charley stayed outside. He would sit in the car, waiting for Mass to be over to drive Anna home. Inside, Anna would pray that someday Charley would become a Catholic.

That first year I was in the parish, I would often see Charley parked just outside the front door of the church. When I wasn't presiding at the Mass, I would often walk over to greet the parishioners after Mass. Every now and then on the way to church I'd stop at Charley's car. Charley and I would chat about the weather or baseball or the family. He was always gracious, with a gentle smile that lingered long after I'd said, "Take care, Charley" and went to greet the parishioners. Every so often, especially if the weather were cold, I'd invite Charley to come inside and wait for Anna in the back of church.

Then to my surprise, one September Charley showed up at the first session of those interested in joining the church. Anna's prayers had been answered. Charley was becoming a Catholic. With Anna by his side, Charley never missed a session during those nine months leading up to his full communion with the church which we celebrated at the Easter Vigil. On that night, with Anna next to him, surrounded by all of his children, grandchildren and great grandchildren, Charley could not contain the joy he felt in his heart. I will never forget the look on Charley Fox's face that night. Joy took on a new name for me that night; it's name was Charley Fox.

Several years later I happened to be in the area again to give a retreat at a nearby parish. Just before the retreat was set to begin, I received a call from Charley's son. He told me he had planned to bring Charley and Anna to the retreat but that after lunch that Sunday afternoon

Charley had sat down in his easy chair, and died. His son asked if I could have Charley's funeral.

At his funeral, I told his family what I just wrote: about the look on Charley's face the night he joined the church. The look on his face spelled Easter for me. I told them stories about Charley I had heard from family and friends earlier that week, stories about a man who found faith late in life but who was found by God the day he was born. I told stories of faith, of friendship, of favor that tried to capture the life Charley Fox lived. It was a life well lived that his baptism only underscored.

Then, after communion at his funeral, one of his sons and some of his grandchildren got up and told more stories. His son said, "I never had any problem telling my mom that I love her, but I never felt comfortable saying it to Dad. So, Dad, here goes: I love you." He proceeded to sing his father's favorite song.

In one man and in many memories, we celebrated Charley Fox's life on earth and ritualized his birth to eternal life.

RITUAL STORYTELLING: WAKING THE DEAD

When we gather to remember a person who has died, we call it a wake service. This is what we seek to do: We try to wake the dead with the stories of their fidelity and friendship. The name of the one who has died is carried in every syllable, every sentence. We tell the stories to keep the dead one's spirit alive in our minds, our hearts, our memories. We do this because we believe that death has no power over us. We do this because we believe in life, not death.

Waking the dead: It's a perfect time to tell the stories one more time. I remember the wake of a man named John. He had had a fascination with trains as a child, but being raised in a mining town he was expected to go work in the mines. The first day he was in the coal mine there was a cave-in. Everyone got out, but the experience convinced John that he would enjoy working on the railroad a lot more. So he became a watchman. Stories at his wake service focused on his penchant for timekeeping. He knew the value of time. One man said, "Now he has boarded the train destined for glory." This is the stuff of wake stories. It's stuff that sticks in peoples' minds like overcooked pasta clings to the wall. Storytelling lets the memories of loved ones dry on the walls of our souls.

We wake the dead with our stories and theirs. Though they sleep in death, their memories remain awake in us. We tell these stories to trace the meaning of our lives, to discover again why we are here, what difference we have made and where we go from here.

We ritualize these memories not only in stories but in symbols. For example, we often place items that held special significance for the one who has died near the casket. One of the most memorable wake services I've ever attended was for a brother in my religious community. Brother Carl Mueller had been the cook at the seminary where I went to high school, and later the cook at the house where I lived for several years. He died quite suddenly of a stroke at the age of fifty. Brother Carl was a great cook and an exceptional baker. His cinnamon rolls and homemade bread were legendary. So, at this wake service the last loaf of bread that Brother Carl had baked was placed near his casket. Then, after many of his friends came forward to tell stories of his life, the person leading the wake service invited all those present to enjoy a piece of Brother Carl's bread. The church was crowded with more than three hundred people, but with each person taking a small morsel that loaf was shared by all the people who were there that night. Each of us savored the flavor of Brother Carl's bread one last time. It was a ritual moment that nourished our souls.

RITUALS OF TAKING LEAVE

Our challenge is to ritualize the landmark moments of our lives in the context of our communal worship. For example, when members of the parish have to move out of town because of job or family considerations, do we allow them to slip out the back door and disappear into the darkness without saying good-bye? I believe it is important to develop rituals for leave-taking: to gather as a community, a family of faith, and tell the stories one more time. Such leave-taking rituals might include toasting our friendship and sending forth the ones who are leaving with a blessing and a kiss of peace.

Family rituals of taking leave, as when a son or a daughter goes away to college, are important mile-markers of life's passages. A letter from parents or a familiar memento from home can be carried on the journey to remind the college student of the sacred connection with family.

Going-away parties provide a ritual that gives parameters to one's past, present and future. Saying farewell through rituals assures that no matter how far one may travel, this place and these people will always be there in the one space that matters most — our heart's memory.

When a brother in our religious community left a place where he'd been for more than a decade, he pleaded with the people not to have a party or do anything special. I understood his penchant for privacy, his not wanting to be the center of attention and his fear of not being able to control his emotions at a farewell party, but he denied the people — and himself — a ritual opportunity to mark his passage to another place.

PAY ATTENTION TO RITUAL ACTION

We've all been involved in such ritualizing. What I'm suggesting is not new. Perhaps our key consideration in the art of ritual is to **pay attention**. Pay attention to the moment. Don't take it for granted. For when we take a ritual action for granted, it is deadly. Just think of our celebration of the Eucharist. We've all participated in Masses that have seemed lifeless or Masses where the medium seemed more important than the message, the meaning, the memory. In such cases performance seems to prevent the full participation of those involved. When rituals become either too routine, too rehearsed or too affected, they lose their power of meaning.

For rituals to have an impact they must reflect the lived experience of those involved. No matter how often we have been involved in a specific ritual action, we are charged with the responsibility of making them fresh and ever new, as if we are doing them for the very first time.

When we ritualize, we're wise not to be concerned so much with the "rightness" of how rituals conform to certain rules or rubrics, but rather with the "rightness" of how they capture the experience of our ongoing conversion. We need to leave room for spontaneity, for the Spirit is very spontaneous.

For rituals to linger in our memory, they should be well-planned but not prepackaged. We really don't care, do we, when we are in the company of friends, if some particular part of the ritual doesn't work out quite as well as we had planned? I remember an Easter Vigil when, during the reading of the Genesis account, slides of nature and scenes of creation were shown. However, the person running the projector was a couple of slides behind the one telling the story. So when the words, "And God created the man," were spoken, a picture of a jackass came on the screen! The laughter seemed appropriate to me since the basic truth of what we were celebrating that night — the resurrection of Jesus — was God's everlasting laugh on the forces of death.

Rituals mark the milestones of our lives. When one's life journey takes him or her in a different direction, rituals of leave-taking commemorate that person's life and love. They help us move on, confident that though the future may take us to different and distant places our unity is found in truth not in time, in spirit not in space, in love not in the limits of geography or history.

A Matter of Revival

Ritualizing those links of love in our lives is necessary for the revival of our spirits. I recall a story Sr. Jose Hobday told about growing up in the 1930s. Even though her family was not desperately poor, they were poor enough to always be living on the edge of insecurity.

One Saturday evening when she was a young girl, she was working on her homework in the living room. Her brothers were outside with friends. Her parents were in the kitchen discussing their financial situation. Her mom and dad were talking about what bills had to be paid and how there wasn't enough money. As Jose listened, she became anxious as she heard about the school needs, fuel bills, food costs.

Suddenly the conversation ended. Her mother came into the living room and put money on the table where Jose was sitting. "Here," her mother said. "Go find your brothers and run to the drugstore before it closes. Use the money to buy some ice cream."

Jose was astonished. She objected. This money should be used to pay some bills, she told her mother. She went into the kitchen to plead her case to her dad. But her father looked at her, threw his head back and laughed. "Your mother is right, honey," he said. "When we get this worried about a few dollars, we are better off having nothing at all. We can't solve all the problems, so maybe we should celebrate what we have. Now, do what your mother says."

So, she gathered up her brothers, and they brought back arms full of ice cream. Her mother made some cookies and coffee. Her dad went to the neighbors and invited them to come over. They had a great party.

This was a ritual moment of survival — the survival of the spirit. To this day Sr. Jose doesn't remember what happened to all the other needs the family had, but she will always remember the freedom and fun of that evening.

It was not only a matter of survival; it was a matter of revival. There is enough pain in our world to go around. There is enough pain in our personal lives to keep us down. There are enough problems to shatter our security, enough tragedy to terrorize our souls. Some of us may see all the problems and be tempted to lose hope. We may give in to the attitude of being defeated. We look for answers but often come up empty. Such fear and hopelessness can only lead to building barriers, fortifying our defenses, keeping us apart.

Our participation in the reign of God demands that we be people who are not only about survival but about revival. To revive means to breathe new life into tired and aching hearts, bodies, spirits. It means that when the wind has been knocked out of us, when we are out of breath and out of answers, we rely on each other and on God to revive us. One way to do this is to create rituals that reminds us that God's spirit still stirs among us.

Pass It On

One individual who was deeply committed to this revival was the late Sr. Thea Bowman. She was a diamond in the rough terrain of world events, a light in the dangerous darkness of despair. A few years ago in St. Louis I had the privilege of hearing her speak. Her body was already racked by the cancer that would ultimately take her life. She spoke to us from a wheelchair. Though her body was held down, her spirit soared beyond any imposed limitations. She was on fire and she enkindled fire in us. She kept identifying us not as priests, brothers, sisters, lay men or women, but as church.

Thea Bowman taught everyone from poor children to rich bishops what it means to be church. She was a proclamation of joy. Her commitment was contagious. She described herself as an "old folks' child" in reference to the basic Christian values she learned from the wise elders of her African-American community.

"The elders in my church and the elders in my community made a deliberate effort to teach me about life," she said. "To teach me about love. To teach me about happiness and joy. To teach me how to deal with my insecurity and to convince me that I was somebody special." They would tell her: If you know how to cook, then teach somebody; if you know how to sew, then teach somebody; if you know how to read, then teach somebody; if you know how to raise a child, if you know how to get and hold a job, then teach somebody.

What you know, Thea Bowman said, is not given to you to sit on. It is given to you so you can pass it on.

That is our challenge as well. To pass on to the next generation the rituals of hope, love and joy that reflect the face of God.

From playing pinochle at a family feast to saying good-bye to those we love, from hand-me-down clothes to ice cream on a Saturday night, from tape-recording the tales of our lives to pass on to our children to recording on our minds the words of Jesus, "Do this in memory of me" (Luke 22: 19), rituals evoke the sacred bonds that make us who we are. They etch images of love on our hearts and minds and memories.

Rituals provide us with the language of hope. They mark our past, celebrate our present and give us the courage to believe in the future.

Rituals, in the words of a friend, offer fresh bread to stale lives. So break some fresh-baked bread and pour some vintage wine in the company of friends and discover the hope within you.

The hope that is God.

HOME AT LAST: THE PILGRIMS' PARABLE

Chapter Twelve

We shall not cease from exploration.
And the end of all our exploring
Will be to arrive where we started
And know the place for the first time.

— T.S. Eliot

Everywhere I go, I find a poet has been there before me.

— Sigmund Freud

We have come a long way, and we are very close to the end of our trail. The journey of transformation has taken us down many winding roads, around perilous curves, to the tops of mountains and through valleys where death has stalked us like a shadow. Throughout the journey, we have stopped to rest, to reflect and to rendezvous with God, who is revealed in the creation, incarnation and redemption stories of our lives. On this last leg of our journey through the heartland, we sense how close we are to that place where all of life finds its basic truth, the place we call home.

We are so close, in fact, that we have the urge to run the last mile. But there is one more place we have to visit. Though it is on the way home, it may seem at first like an out-of-the-way place. It also may feel as if we've been to this place before. In a sense, we have. We visited this place when we were children and our parents would tell us a story before turning out the lights and wishing us good night. It's the place where some of the fairy tales we were told as children were set because of its magic and its mystery. This place is a forest. Here the truths of our creation, incarnation and redemption stories are revealed once again. In this parable of two pilgrims, a poet and a prophet who make several rest stops deep in the woods, we will discover the wisdom and the wonder this journey of the soul has awakened in us. We will find the wisdom and wonder of the true meaning of home found in those eloquent words of the poet, T.S. Eliot:

> We shall not cease from exploration.
> And the end of all our exploring
> Will be to arrive where we started
> And know the place for the first time.

A long time ago in a forest far, far away, an epic journey unfolded. We revisit this scene of a poet and a prophet walking in the woods late one winter's afternoon. The breeze is playing ever so lightly upon the bare branches of the trees. Every now and then a creature hidden beneath damp leaves stirs and gnaws at the silence.

As the sun goes down, the wind begins to prowl. The poet turns to the prophet and says, "Better get out the torch, fair prophet, or we will never find our way home."

"Torch?" the prophet replies. "I thought you brought the torch."

"You mean to tell me you didn't bring the torch?"

"No. I thought *you* brought the torch."

"I brought *my lyre* to play by the fire which was going to be lit by the torch *you* brought," the poet says. "What are we going to do now? It will be dark soon, and we don't have a clue as to where we are."

"Not to worry," the prophet says. "You know the saying, 'There's nothing new under the sun'? So maybe we should try the moon! For under the light of the winter's moon we may be able to find our way in the dark."

Night falls silently as the two pilgrims walk slowly, cautiously, through the woods, unaware of the stories the darkness will hide in her shadows. "The moon is not so bright as to illuminate the secrets of this night," the poet says as they inch along.

The prophet smiles. "Ah, she's not so bright, but she knows enough."

Time passes slowly as the darkness thickens. They feel their way through the foliage of the forest until, in the distance, they notice the light of a cabin. As they approach the cabin in the clearing, they see that the light is actually several glowing candles — a menorah — sitting in the window. The smell of wood burning in a fireplace beckons them to warm themselves by the fire inside. The poet, the more spontaneous of the two, knocks on the door.

An old woman answers. "Welcome, weary pilgrims," she says. "Welcome to my home. You've come on just the right night. It is the feast of Hanukkah, the festival of lights. I would enjoy the favor of your company this night. For this, the darkest night of the year, is not one to spend alone. Come, friends, warm yourselves by the fire."

As the old woman pours some tea and warms some soup, she tells her guests how tradition holds that Hanukkah celebrates the triumph of the few over the many, the remnant over the mighty, the weak over the strong. "This is the night," she says, "when we dedicate our humble dwellings as our ancestors dedicated the temple. This is the night when magic and miracles create marvels our hearts long to hold. This night, your presence in my humble home blesses this dwelling and makes it holy."

As the poet and prophet sip their tea and slurp their soup, the old woman tells a winter's tale:

Legend has it that in this forest there is a dark cave down in the ground, deep down under the earth. This cave had never seen the light, and so did not know what light was. But one day, the sun invited the cave to come up and visit. When the cave came up to visit the sun, it was amazed and delighted because the cave had never seen light before. Well, naturally, the cave felt obligated and invited the sun to come down underground to visit it sometime. The sun was intrigued by the invitation since the sun had never seen the darkness.

So the day arrived, and the sun came down and was ushered into the cave. The sun looked around and, puzzled, asked, "Where is the darkness?" For when the sun came down to earth, the darkness disappeared. On such a dark and damp night long ago, light was invited into a cramped cave. And the darkness disappeared.

The poet and the prophet sit pondering the old woman's story as they warm their feet by the fire. The question, "Where is the darkness" hangs in the air like incense in the old woman's cabin on this cold winter's night. Just before the poet gives way to sleep, he reflects on the familiar words sparked by the woman's story. They are the first words, in fact, attributed to God in the book of Genesis: "Let there be light."

The next morning as the poet and prophet prepare to leave, the old woman invites them to stand by the door. She places a hand on both of their heads and prays a blessing. Then, from a weathered-looking wooden box she takes two sun broaches and hangs one around the neck of each pilgrim. "Wear this sun broach close to your heart," she says, "so that when the darkness fills your journey you will remember to invite the sun into the cave of your heart and dispel the darkness. Go in peace. And remember, 'Let there be light.'"

Guided by the sun's journey across the sky, the poet and prophet continue their journey through the forest. A few days later, they arrive at another hermitage. There they are greeted by a generous smile on the face of an old man. "I have been waiting for you, good pilgrims," the old man says. "Please, come in and rest your weary bodies." After preparing a light lunch for the poet and prophet, the old man asks if they want to take a nap. Both are eager for sleep and so the old man places two rugs near the back wall of the cabin. The accommodations, however, are not quite complete. The old man proceeds to nail a hoop containing feathers and beads to the wall above each of the rugs. Both hoops are woven like a spider's web with a hole in the center of the circle.

"What is the meaning of this hooped web?" the poet asks.

"Ah, let me tell you about it in a story before you sleep." As the prophet and poet sit on the rugs, the old hermit spins this tale:

According to an ancient Lakota legend, when the world was young, there was a wise, spiritual elder of the people who went to a high mountain and entertained a vision. In this vision, Iktomi, the great teacher of wisdom, appeared to the elder as a spider. Speaking to the spiritual leader in a sacred language only the elders of the Lakota could understand, Iktomi reflected on the cycles of life. As Iktomi spoke, the spider took the willow hoop of the elder which had feathers, horse hair, beads and offerings on it and began to spin a web.

"We begin our lives as infants," Iktomi said. "Then we move to childhood, adolescence and then adulthood. Finally, we move to old age where we are taken care of as infants once again. And the cycle is complete."

As the spider continued to spin the web, Iktomi said: "But in each cycle of life there are dreams, both good and bad, that guide you. If you listen to the good dreams, they will lead you in the right direction, the path of goodness and holiness. But if you take the bad dreams to heart, they will hurt you and guide in you in a direction of evil. There are so many dreams and so many different directions one's life can take. These dreams either enable or impede the wonderful teachings of the Great Spirit."

As the spider continued to speak, the strands of the web took shape, starting from the outside of the hoop and working their way toward the center. When the web was complete, Iktomi gave the hoop to the elder and said, "You see, this web is a perfect circle. But notice how in the center of the circle there is a hole."

"What is the meaning of this hole?" the elder asked.

"Place this web above the place where you sleep," Iktomi advised. "Allow this web to help you and your people reach your dreams. If you believe in the Great Spirit, this web will catch your good dreams. And the bad dreams will go through the hole and disappear."

When the Lakota elder came down from the mountain, he shared his vision with his people. Each member of the community created a web and placed it above their beds. This dream catcher became the symbol for sifting through their dreams and visions. Their good dreams were caught in the web of life and were carried with them. But their evil dreams escaped through the hole in the center and disappeared from their lives forever.

The people believed that this dream catcher, this web of life, captured their destiny.

"Rest now, pilgrim friends," the old man says after completing the story. "And as you sleep, don't forget to dream."

Two hours later, the poet and prophet awaken, refreshed by the rest and ready to continue their journey. As they bid their gracious host farewell, the old hermit gives each of them a dream catcher. "As you walk in the forest, gentle pilgrims, don't be afraid to dream."

As the poet and prophet continue their journey through the forest, the days grow longer and the nights warmer. They listen to the sounds of frogs chanting an anthem of welcome to nature's rebirth. They often stop to notice how the gray limbs of trees are gradually taking on some green. Hope fills their hearts, and spring returns to their step. At one point, however, the poet says, "You know, good prophet, we still don't know where we are. Thus far we have relied on the sun, stars and moon to give us a sense of direction, but soon the trees of the forest will be in full flower and will block our view. Perhaps it's time to take out your compass."

"You are right, good friend," the prophet says. "Let us sit a spell, and I will check my knapsack for the compass. Ah, here it is."

The poet frowns. "That, my friend, is a compass for making circles, not for going places."

"But this is the only compass I brought, the only compass I ever use," the prophet says. "After all, it is my call to make larger and larger circles wherever I go."

"Ah," the poet replies, "but with such a compass you stay in the same place. With the other kind of compass we'd be able to check our direction and travel with a measure of confidence that even if we don't know exactly where we're going we'll be heading in the right direction."

"Do you think we've been going in circles since we started this journey? If so, dear poet, I beg to differ. For look over there in the clearing — yet another cabin that is beckoning us as guests!"

They knock on the door of the cabin, but there is no response. After a more forceful blow, the door swings open. "Peace to this house!" the poet shouts. "Is anyone home?" The cabin is sparsely furnished and dusty. "It seems no one has called this 'home' for some time," the prophet muses.

As they look around the cabin, the poet notices a small, silver container on the table near the window. When he opens it, he sees it is a compass for checking directions. Slipping the silver case into his vest pocket, the poet says, "Come, good friend, it's time to go."

Before they can leave the cabin, however, a young man appears at the door. "May I help you?" he asks.

The poet, rarely at a loss for words, is so startled by the sudden appearance of the young man that he is speechless. "Excuse us," the prophet says, "we are so very sorry for this intrusion. We thought the cabin was abandoned."

"Hello! What is it you want?"

Sensing the young man is not upset at finding strangers in his house, the poet regains his voice. "We were looking for directions."

"Where are you going? Maybe I can help. I've lived in this forest all my life and know the land well."

Since the truth is always at the tip of the prophet's tongue, he says, "We don't know exactly where we are going."

"I've been there too," the young man says with a wink.

For the next couple of hours, the poet and prophet tell the young man the stories of where they have been, about the old woman and the old man they have met and the gifts of the sun broach and dream catcher they have received.

The young man in turn tells them how he spends most of his days and nights wandering in the forest. "I am a pilgrim at heart," he says. "That is why this cabin has very little furniture. Though I sleep here now and then, I don't need much. After all, I'm just passing through. There is, however, one thing I do collect: stories. If you're not in a hurry — and since you don't know where you're going I suspect you have a little time — do you mind if I share a story with you?"

The poet and prophet smile at each other. "Please," the poet says, "gift us with a story."

One day as I was wandering far into the forest, I came to a place that looked familiar. It was a salvage shop with a sign that said, "Gus and Son" hanging by one rusted chain above the door. I walked inside this cluttered store and saw antiques I'd seen before. There was a tent folded up in the corner, and the musty smell reminded me of camping out with my friends when I was a boy. Behind some dusty plates with a *Currier and Ives* winter scene etched upon them — a scene I recognized from years before when I was told to eat everything on my plate or I couldn't go outside to play — I saw an old baseball glove. The glove was worn and tied together with string, but it fit my hand so well I didn't want to take it off. I could see the pride in my dad's eyes when I used this glove to snare a line drive destined for center field.

Over in the corner I noticed a bookshelf. I found a copy of

Huckleberry Finn with a torn cover and a page-worn manuscript of *Walden Pond*. I remembered how I wanted to write books of adventure and solitude, and I wondered why I never had.

In the case by the cash register I saw an autograph book. Since the case was unlocked, I reached in and read the names and promises scribbled on the yellow pages. "I will miss you," one said, and the name "Mary Ann" sparked a memory and a face.

I was tempted to buy a few things, but the owner said, "It's all free — take what you want." Although I left empty-handed, when I started walking away I felt a vague notion of a place called *home*.

Finishing the story, the young man looks at the poet, "Please keep the compass. You will need it to find your way home." The poet blushes. "Go in peace," the young man says, "and have a good trip."

Like the poet and the prophet, we are pilgrims who have wandered into a forest. Like that old woman, our God has welcomed us to the heartland's holy ground with a candle in the window and a fire in the hearth. Like that old man, our God has given us a web of community to catch our dreams. And like that young man, our pilgrim God gives us a compass in the form of friends who share this walk in the woods with us.

The parable of the poet and prophet reminds us that only by tracing our tradition, by recalling the stories of our ancestors, by reverencing the stories of those we meet, by drawing upon the wisdom of those who walk with us, will we sense a direction for our lives. Though we walk at times through new and perhaps unfamiliar territory, certain signs along the journey found in its stories and symbols will show us the way.

For the first disciples of Jesus, certainly the resurrection was unfamiliar territory. During the Easter season, we hear stories of how the first followers of Jesus didn't recognize his risen presence right away. For example, we recall how the disciples on the road to Emmaus didn't recognize the one who joined them on the road until he stopped at their house for dinner. At that famous Emmaus rest stop, in the midst of telling a few stories, he broke some bread. Perhaps the reality of the resurrection, the real presence, was so close the disciples just couldn't see — until they stopped along the road. Later they would say they felt their hearts on fire — like flames coming through the cracks of their broken hearts. However, they wouldn't see the real presence until not only their hearts were broken but their bread too.

Like the story of Emmaus, the story of the poet and the prophet suggests that only when our hearts and bread are broken will we see the real presence of the Risen One on this path of life. We will touch the Risen One in gifts we receive along the way. We will hear the Risen One in stories of those who welcome us. We will sense the Risen One in salvage shops where we stop along the way, shops that are filled with memories of our youth we can't reclaim but must never forget.

As we continue the journey of transformation, we carry with us all the stories of all the pilgrims who have walked and prayed along the way. The gift of their companionship is a sun broach which hangs close to our heart reminding us that whenever or wherever the darkness descends there is a light within that will show us the way. Their friendship is like a dream catcher that captures all our dreams and gives us a future. Their presence in our lives is like a compass that gives us direction as our journey continues.

Whenever we huddle close in prayer at the rest stops of the soul and share the stories, we discover the truth that we are home at last.

At day's end
all our footsteps are added up
to see how near.

         – W. S. Merwin, "Last People"

THE LAST REST STOP: GRATITUDE

I have been blessed to experience the soulful stories of many people at various rest stops along the way. When I was a student living in Kansas City, an important rest stop was the card table at Patty and Dick Bishop's house. When I moved to St. Joseph, Missouri, for my first foray into public ministry, it was the kitchen table at Steve and Conny Swymeler's. In Centerville, Iowa, it was the back porch at Lucy and Rollie Reznicek's and the living room in the home of Adrian and Lorraine Ramos. When I journeyed to Davenport for a year, Patti Hoffman provided the rest stop where I drew inspiration and encouragement. In 1985, I moved to Sedalia, Missouri, where numerous people provided rest stops. They know who they are, but I especially want to thank Mary K. and Bret Williams and Barb and Frank Wetteroth, whose back yard on summer Sunday afternoons was the perfect place to listen to Cardinal games and play Whiffleball.

Since 1969, members and companions of the Precious Blood Congregation have shaped so much of my soul. I am grateful to all of them, especially to Father Mark Miller, my religious superior, whom I am privileged to have as a good friend, and Fathers Vince Hoying and Mike Volkmer, whose priestly service is beyond compare.

I am grateful to the staff of Shantivanam, the House of Prayer for the Archdiocese of Kansas City in Kansas, for their encouragement, support and challenge. For more than twenty-five years, Shantivanam has offered a sacred space for solitude and prayer. I am deeply indebted to all the present and former staff members whose care, prayer and hospitality has offered so many spiritual pilgrims a rest stop for the soul. I am grateful as well to Archbishop Ignatius Strecker, whose vision and invitation to Father Ed Hays to establish this house of prayer made this dream a reality, and to Archbishop James Keleher whose support continues to nurture the vitality of Shantivanam, the Forest of Peace. To all the guests and generous friends of this forest who make this rest stop possible, I am deeply grateful.

This book would not be in your hands if it were not for the encouragement, expertise and friendship of Tom Turkle, my publisher, Tom Skorupa, my editor, and all the staff at Forest of Peace Publishing who provide such rich resources for those on the spiritual journey.

As I pulled together these reflections this past year, good friends have provided places and spaces in their hearts where the stories could be told and I could find some rest for my soul. My thanks to Tren Meyers, Sister Mary V. Maronick, Chris Ostmeyer, Josie LeCluyse, Phyllis DeMey, Tom and Beth Jacobs, and Deb Patyrak.

Finally, to my mom and dad, Doris and Joe Nassal, who on May 1, 1998, will celebrate their fiftieth wedding anniversary — I will always be grateful to you for providing the original rest stop, a place to call home.